GRASSES

AND

BAMBOOS

Using form and shape to create visual impact in the garden

GRASSES AND BAMBOOS

NOËL KINGSBURY

with photography by ANDREA JONES
consultant PAUL WHITTAKER

RYLAND
PETERS
& SMALL
LONDON NEW YORK

First published in Great Britain
in 2000 by Ryland Peters & Small
Kirkman House
12-14 Whitfield Street
London W1T 2RP

10 9 8 7 6 5 4 3 2

Designer Sailesh Patel
Senior Designer Paul Tilby
Senior Editor Sian Parkhouse
Production Meryl Silbert
Art Director Gabriella Le Grazie
Publishing Director Anne Ryland

www.rylandpeters.com

Printed in China.

ISBN 1 84172 043 7

A catalogue record for this book is
available from the British Library

PAGE 1: *Carex comans*
PAGES 2–3: Piet Oudolf's garden (top)
PAGE 4: *Miscanthus sinensis* 'Morning Light'
PAGE 5: *Chimonobambusa tumidissionoda*

CONTENTS

INTRODUCTION

GRASSES, AND THE RELATED SEDGES
AND RUSHES, HAVE MUCH TO OFFER
THE GARDENER: A LONG SEASON OF
ELEGANT GROWTH AND A TOUGHNESS
AND RESILIENCE THAT MAKES THEM
EXCEPTIONALLY USEFUL, ESPECIALLY
FOR SITES EXPOSED TO THE
ELEMENTS. BUT THERE IS MORE THAN
THIS TO GRASSES — THERE IS ALSO
AN INTIMATE RELATIONSHIP WITH
HUMAN HISTORY THAT MAKES THEM
PARTICULARLY IMPORTANT TO US.

OPPOSITE: A variegated bamboo, *Sasaella masamuneana f. albostriata* is
the highlight of this arrangement of plants. The bamboo to the left is
Sasa kurilensis (dwarf form) and in front is *Carex morrowii* 'Variegata'.

ABOVE: *Phyllostachys bambusoides* 'Castillonis' is one of many bamboos
with canes of great beauty.

Grass is one of the most all-pervasive and dominant features of plant life on planet earth, and, as lawn, perhaps the most widely grown garden plant. Yet it is only recently that grasses have become widespread in gardens, other than bamboos or lawn grasses. Gardeners and landscape architects the world over are now waking up to the fact that grasses are extraordinarily versatile, resilient and ornamental plants for a vast number of situations, from tiny backyards to the sweeping grounds of corporate headquarters.

Firstly, we need to look at what exactly grass is, at the role it plays in the world and at its history, then put it in context. The grass family (Gramineae) is a botanical division comprising some 10,000 species, which includes the 1,000-strong subfamily of woody grasses known as bamboos, the majority of which are tropical. But there are also many other plants, superficially similar, but which are not botanically classified as grasses because of the different nature of their flowers, the basis of scientific classification of plants. In this book I include sedges (Cyperaceae) and rushes (Juncaceae), which not only look like grasses but behave like them, covering large areas in their growth, a matrix for other plant species. There are also others, known as grass-like plants, that are not grasses and which do not form this matrix-type vegetation, but which are used as grasses in horticulture. In this book, 'grasses' is understood to mean true grasses, sedges and rushes, but not 'grass-like plants'.

It is the matrix quality that develops from the way that many grasses grow that has enabled them to cover so much of the world, forming the vast grasslands that have played such a crucial role in human history. Geologically speaking, grasses are young plants, having evolved only 36 million years ago, whereas the first conifersappeared some 400 million years ago, for example . They have a more efficient method of photosynthesis than other plants, enabling them to grow in the declining levels of carbon dioxide that have been a feature of the history of life on earth (until human pollution at any rate).

One reason grasses can form such a tight blanket of growth is their flowers are wind pollinated; they do not have to rely on insects to fertilize them to produce seed, enabling them to spread rapidly and consistently. It is these flower heads, turning as the season advances into seed heads, that gives so many grasses their distinctively attractive character. But there are two separate

LEFT: Often mistakenly called bulrushes, the reedmaces (*Typha* species) are important waterside plants.

ABOVE: Surface features, such as pleating, are an attractive aspect of many bamboos.

OPPOSITE: Pampas grass, *Cortaderia selloana*, is seen through a transparent screen created by another grass.

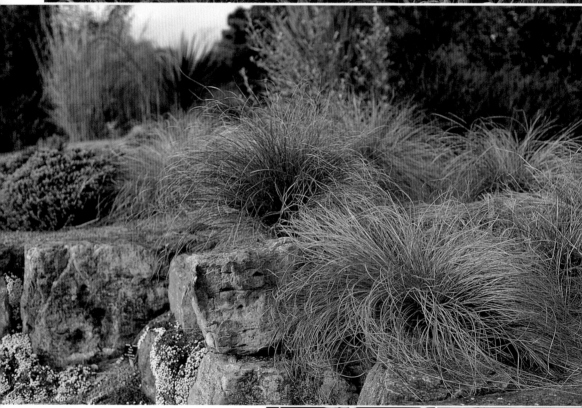

TOP: *Miscanthus* varieties are guarded by pots of the feathery *Pennisetum villosum*.

ABOVE: *Carex buchananii* is one of many New Zealand sedges with year-round colour.

RIGHT: Many of the *Panicum* species are native to the American prairie.

CENTRE RIGHT: *Molinia caerulea* ssp. *arundinacea* has fine flower and seed heads.

FAR RIGHT: *Typha laxmannii* is a reedmace.

habits of growth that have a major effect on how they grow and on the way they can be used in the garden. Turf or sod-forming grasses produce runners, enabling them to rapidly cover ground without producing seeds. Most species native to cool temperate climates are of this kind, and it is this quality we put to use in lawns. Few such species make good ornamental plants for borders, as they run invasively. In harsher climates, clump-forming grasses dominate, proving their value and stress tolerance in our gardens; they form non-spreading clumps or tussocks, which abut each other closely, but leave more space in between for other plant species. They tend to be both more decorative as individual plants and more suitable in the garden. There are also a small number of annual species, including the decorative *Briza maxima*, the quaking grass.

The vast majority of grass species are from environments where climatic extremes such as cold or drought prevent tree growth, which is the predominant form of vegetation over most of the world. Before the arrival of humans, grasslands would naturally have been restricted to land above the tree line, coasts, and those regions, usually in the centre of continents, with severe seasonal drought.

Human history, even our development as a species, has been intimately tied up with grasses. We evolved in the African savannah, a habitat of scattered trees and stretches of wildlife-rich grassland. It is possible that early humans soon learned that fire destroys trees, or at least stops them regenerating. It thus assists the formation of grasslands, which could then support large herds of grazing animals, which in turn prevent tree seedlings from re-establishing themselves. The prairies of North America were once limited to seasonally dry areas, but were enlarged by nomadic hunters anxious for more space for the buffalo on which they depended for food.

The vast areas of natural and semi-natural grassland that cover many of those parts of the globe which have a seasonally dry climate have been an ideal home for the development of nomadic peoples who have followed herds of animals, either wild or domestic. The grasslands of Central Asia have supported such a lifestyle for many thousands of years – a lifestyle which is generally a very productive one, allowing populations to build up. In drought years, though, the threat of famine leads to mass movements of men and animals. The

TOP: La Bambouseraie in south-east France is an exceptional collection of bamboos.

ABOVE: *Miscanthus sinensis* 'Kleine Fontäne' and *Deschampsia cespitosa* 'Goldtau' feature in one of Dutch designer Piet Oudolf's borders. BELOW: Bamboos thrive in the foothills of Mount Fuji, Japan.

OPPOSITE: Bamboos and grasses take different forms: the yellow canes of *Phyllostachys aureosulcata* 'Spectabilis' contrast with *Calamagrostis* x *acutiflora* 'Karl Foerster' and *Stipa tenuifolia* (below).

history of Europe, the Muslim Middle East, and especially China, has been punctuated by periodical outbursts of horse-riding warriors from the grasslands, whose highly mobile way of life and warfare made them formidable opponents for populations dependent upon crops for their livelihood. Some, such as Attila the Hun and Genghis Khan, were savage and destructive; most however were more peaceable or more ready to learn from the settled agricultural nations they had invaded, such as the Germanic tribes or the Turks. It is hardly surprising grass has followed human history. Grass feeds the cattle and other animals that are the mainstay of agricultural economies. All cereals are grasses too. Fields and pastures have become the norm over vast areas where once the forest held sway.

Pervasive as it is now, the use of grass as an ornamental plant is a relatively late arrival onto the horticultural scene. The enclosed villa gardens of the Romans, the courtyard gardens of Islam and medieval European monastic gardens had no space for lawns – although medieval knights and their lovers enjoyed the delights of the 'flowery mead', this would have been no more than a wildflower meadow within easy reach of the castle walls. Grass made an appearance in Tudor times, for sports such as bowls, but did not become a major part of the garden until the 17th century, when landowners began to lay out extensive grounds. Lawn grass became the foreground to the *allées* and statuary of French master gardener André Le Notre and, later on, rougher cattle-grazed pasture became an essential part of the 'English style'; whole landscapes were made into a romanticized Arcadia comprising clumps of trees, lakes and rolling green hills.

Lawn grass was here to stay, but it had to be cut, on the larger scale with sheep or on a smaller scale with teams of workers armed with scythes. A lawn was something of a status symbol, as one had to either have enough land to have sheep or be able to employ staff to scythe. It was not until the invention of the mechanical lawnmower in the 19th century that it was possible for more people to have their own lawns, which were soon *de rigueur* for the expanding middle classes of Europe and North America.

RIGHT: *Luzula nivea*, a woodrush, is glimpsed through a haze of blue campanula.

BELOW: Species of *Typha* thrive in a typical waterside habitat.

BOTTOM, CLOCKWISE FROM TOP LEFT: Grasses and bamboos in all their variety: *Carex sylvatica*; *Nassella trichotoma*; *Sasa veitchii*; *Phyllostachys aurea* 'Holochrysa'.

While some gardening magazines of the 1880s mention using grasses as ornamental plants, there was little interest in them. Foliage plants may have been popular as house plants but it seemed as if the lack of flower colour in grasses condemned them to the margins of the garden. The bold colours of perennials, sub-tropical bedding plants and the increasing number of exuberant flowering shrubs introduced from the East, such as camellias and rhododendrons, attracted far more attention.

Though the Japanese have a long tradition of using grasses in containers, usually accompanying bonsai, in the West, interest in ornamental grasses really got under way in post-war Germany, when nurseryman, designer and writer Karl Foerster began to use them in naturalistic compositions alongside perennials. He recognized their value as plants with a long season of interest, even through harsh winter weather. Richard Hansen, who was also German, worked on a study of perennials in public places, using grasses as accompaniments to conventional flowering plants. Gardeners in other countries then started to use them, with particular interest in the United States. Today the leading lights in the use of grasses are Wolfgang Oehme (who trained in Germany in the 1950s) and James van Sweden, in the United States, and Piet Oudolf in the Netherlands. Oehme and van Sweden use them in concentrated blocks, inspired by the prairies of the Midwest, whilst Oudolf creates borders using a dramatic blend of grasses and perennials.

Bamboos are naturally plants of moist temperate forests. They characteristically form understorey vegetation, especially in the tropics (above a certain altitude) and in areas with a warm humid summer. Though they are usually associated with the Far East, there are in fact many species native to Africa and to South America. Some species

BELOW LEFT: Hairgrass, a *Koeleria* species, grows alongside pink knapweed, *Centaurea dealbata*, demonstrating how easily and effectively grasses and bamboos blend with perennials in mixed plantings.

BELOW RIGHT: The fescues are tightly clump-forming grasses, with sharp very narrow evergreen leaves. *Festuca mairei* has a distinct arching style and is suitable for planting in dry places.

cover large areas of ground with impenetrable growth; others climb voraciously, smothering whole trees. They have been in cultivation in the East for centuries, where their elegance has long been recognized, and their utility no doubt for much longer. Bamboo canes combine lightness with strength, making them ideal constructional material; perhaps this is why they are seen as having an important value as the symbol of the relationship between human life and nature.

Bamboo is a favourite subject in Chinese and Japanese art and has long been popular in gardens in both countries; particularly effective use of bamboo is made in Japanese courtyard and temple gardens. Everything in Far Eastern gardens is highly symbolic and representational, with bamboo symbolizing vigour and its canes used to represent forest. Modern Japanese gardens often include non-traditional plants such as yuccas and phormiums alongside bamboo; they are chosen so their foliage presents contrast.

Bamboos were introduced to the West during the 19th century, with particular growth in interest after trade with Japan was established. Many of the first plantings were on large estates, the bamboos being gifts from silk traders to the landowner. Certain extremely invasive species did rather too well in some gardens and the whole group acquired rather a bad reputation. For many years, only a limited number of species have been available commercially, which has also limited their popularity. The more widespread availability of a wider range of species has done much to popularize them, as has a network of enthusiasts throughout Britain, the US and France.

GRASSES HAVE A LIGHTNESS OF
TOUCH UNEQUALLED BY ANY OTHER
GROUP OF PLANTS. IN SEEKING TO
UNDERSTAND HOW THEY CAN BE
USED IN THE GARDEN IT HELPS
TO UNDERSTAND THE QUALITIES THAT
MAKE THEM SPECIAL, ESPECIALLY
SINCE THESE QUALITIES MAY BE
QUITE DIFFERENT FROM THOSE OF
THE MORE CONVENTIONAL GARDEN
PLANTS WE ARE FAMILIAR WITH
IN OUR GARDENS.

QUALITIES

OPPOSITE: A sedge (*Carex* species) lurks in a border, awaiting
its season of glory when everything around it has died down.

ABOVE: *Luzula nivea*, a shade-tolerant evergreen, has a brief
period of flower in early summer.

FORM

This is perhaps the greatest contribution grasses have to make to our gardens. It is an undervalued aspect of plants; far too many people do not see beyond colour. And yet even the most colourful garden can be dull if no attention is paid to the plant forms. It is instructive to take a black-and-white picture of a garden or border, and then see what it has to offer; many colourful plantings are reduced to a jumble of indistinct greys. For much

of the year, there are few flowers in evidence anyway. Rather than give up on the garden altogether, as many do, or just relying on the same few boring evergreens, consider how it might be possible to use a variety of plants with distinctive shapes.

Some grasses, the big and bold ones, can make a definite impression on a large scale. They might be the only grasses in a garden or planting scheme and still be a major presence. A single clump of bamboo or pampas grass (*Cortaderia selloana*) is capable of dominating a large area, 365 days of the year. Equally distinct but smaller grasses, *Calamagrostis* x *acutiflora* 'Stricta', for example, can command a smaller area simply by having a habit, in this case very upright, that is totally distinct from plants around it.

Some gardeners like the stimulating effect of combining lots of different shapes, rather like some people enjoy bringing lots of different colours together, whereas others feel the effect created is too fussy or over stimulating. The former group may well want to mix several different grasses or at least to involve several within a border, counterpoising a variety of different shapes. The latter will probably want to stick to just one or two, to provide structure to a collection of more amorphous plants.

Opinion is divided about combining different grasses, even among enthusiasts. Some feel that they like to keep them separate; others that it is fine to mix different grass varieties. Personally I like to mix them, but to keep it simple, using multiples of two or three species, each with a distinct habit. One of my favourite plantings features the bolt upright *Calamagrostis* x *acutiflora* 'Karl Foerster' surrounded by much lower-growing mound-forming hardy geraniums and a low clump-forming brown sedge (one of the *Carex* species). They contrast brilliantly but do not compete.

Some grasses are deciduous, they live with us for only part of the year, such as the big star burst of *Molinia*; others, such as many *Carex* species, are evergreen and are a permanent feature. Bamboos play a role in the garden not unlike that of evergreen shrubs – they are woody and their structure offers bulk and permanence. One of the most exciting aspects of gardening with grasses is the seasonal dynamism of plant forms: the constant change of deciduous species' growth, death and renewal against a background of permanence.

OPPOSITE: The stiffly upright form of *Calamagrostis* x *acutiflora* 'Karl Foerster' makes it one of the most valuable of all garden grasses.

LEFT: A *Miscanthus* cultivar (left), a bamboo and a *Carex* (front) illustrate the variety of form found among grasses and allied plants.

ABOVE: *Calamagrostis* is one of many grass species that brings life to the late summer garden.

BELOW: *Miscanthus sinensis* 'Sarabande', a reliably flowering cultivar, has narrow elegant leaves.

RIGHT: These almost tree-like canes are those of *Phyllostachys edulis*.

FAR RIGHT: The young growth of bamboos has a much stiffer upright habit than the mature stems. This is yellow-stemmed *Phyllostachys aureosulcata* 'Aureocaulis'.

UPRIGHTS

The majority of garden plants do not have good form; they are often rather shapeless and indistinct. The use of a few strong shapes can transform a garden – and nothing so much as a few good vertical lines, especially in flat areas, or wide open gardens. Grasses provide some of the best verticals you can grow, and are a lot quicker to establish than classic vertical plants such as a palm tree or an Italian cypress.

Close to, tall bamboos, such as *Phyllostachys aurea*, can form wonderful uprights, and they are made great use of in tiny Japanese courtyards, but on the whole bamboos arch too much in cool temperate climates to really stress the vertical. The very tall grasses, such as *Arundo donax* and *Miscanthus sacchariflorus* are certainly impressive, but rather leafy, which can detract from the bold skywards sweep. Any reasonably upright grass, *Cortaderia* or *Miscanthus* for example, makes a good display of vertical thrusting stems for up to half the year, especially given the contrast in colour and line between the stems of the flower/seed heads and the green clumps of leaves.

There are a few grasses, though, that are so superbly upright that the others are quite put in the shade, notably *Calamagrostis* x *acutiflora* 'Stricta' and *C.* x *acutiflora* 'Karl Foerster', which produce bolt-upright flower/seed heads that will last for a good three-quarters of the year, from mid-summer through to early spring. They are completely windproof, being resistant to hurricane-force winds according to James van Sweden, who uses them in coastal gardens on the Atlantic seaboard of the United States. They have small feathery tops on the tall canes, which are very different in effect from the plume-like generally one-sided heads of *Cortaderia* and *Miscanthus*.

Strong verticals in the garden need careful placing and repay considerable thought over grouping. Those that have bulk as well as an upright posture tend to dominate their surroundings, one reason perhaps why *Cortaderia* has become rather unpopular in many quarters. Those that form less of a clump or are more graceful in build are far easier to mix in with others. It is common sense not to have strong vertical lines crowded by other plants at the same height; there seems little doubt that a really good vertical should stand well clear of any surrounding plants, which should be much lower growing.

Having a few clear verticals arising out of other plants can be very dramatic indeed, but some people prefer the effect of a multiple planting. Personally, I feel the two *Calamagrostis* species already mentioned look better planted as single plants that will then grow into small clumps over the years, rather than grown as several massed plants. When they are grown in a large group, I feel that part of the essential qualities of the individual plant is lost. However, I know that certain of my colleagues prefer the sight of massed ranks of upright stems, recalling a reed bed, and grown in this way they certainly act as a good backdrop to lower-growing perennials or groundcover plants. And tall grasses do make very good temporary summer screening or shelter.

ELEGANCE

It is difficult to describe elegance, although we all know it when we see it. Bamboos for many gardeners are the epitome of elegance; it has something to do with the way the stems grow up and then arch over, with the leaves held outward and slightly weeping. The shadows created by bamboo foliage on hard surfaces also have a particular magic. This arching quality seems to be at the heart of the elegance of so many grasses too. Even something as robust as *Carex pendula* with its great clumps of dark green leaves has extremely elegant flowers, long 'catkins' hanging from a long, gently arching stem.

The combination of arching stem and pendent head is a key part of the appeal of many grasses. The comparatively large flower/seed heads of *Chasmanthium latifolium* (syn. *Uniola latifolia*), or of the annual *Briza major*, hanging from thread-like stems, are an example – the latter is known as quaking grass as the heads seem constantly in motion. The plume heads of so many grasses recall the wild reed: they all tend to blow in one direction, with the stems all having exactly the same curvature – a powerful image. A *Miscanthus* on a windy day in early winter is a wonderful example of this. Many of the *Melica* grasses have similar qualities, but on a much more intimate scale.

Elegance and grace are qualities that nearly all the *Stipa* grasses have, whether it is the immensely long awns of *Stipa pennata*, or the tall stems of *Stipa gigantea* with their very open panicles of narrow oat-like heads. It is a quality that always draws attention to itself through its subtlety, and *Stipa gigantea* is certainly subtle. It is undeniably a huge grass, up to two metres tall and wide when in flower, yet it never dominates because its stems are so narrow and so far flung the plant is effectively transparent, and it is possible to see right through it to whatever is behind.

It is the leaves that are the source of grace in some grasses – those with particularly finely shaped leaves, for example, such as many of the *Stipa* species. Even if the leaves themselves are rather coarse in appearance, the way they are arranged around the stem can be especially pleasing to the eye, as in *Spodiopogon sibiricus*.

Elegance is a virtue that needs space to be appreciated. Being such a subtle quality it is easily overwhelmed. Elegant plants should never be cramped, and they should be married with plants or surroundings of quiet beauty. Specimen planting, surrounded by lawn or groundcover, suits some of the larger species, while careful placing is all that others need, so that they are not hidden but are easily seen and thus appreciated.

The traditional Japanese garden, or courtyard, is the perfect place to appreciate elegance and perfection. Fine plants are grown as single specimens, or perhaps a group of several individuals of the same species are planted together, often counterpoised by carefully chosen gravel, stones or timber decking. There is always a contrast of hard and soft textures, straight and curved lines. This is the perfect way to appreciate bamboos, the grace and refinement of practically all parts of all species rewarding close study. Courtyards offer shelter too, much relished by bamboos.

ABOVE FAR LEFT: *Carex pendula* is valuable for bringing its unusual quality of elegance to dry shade.

ABOVE LEFT: The remains of *Spodiopogon sibiricus* seed heads rise above bamboo-like foliage in autumn.

ABOVE: The oat-like panicles of *Stipa gigantea* — it is one of the most widely grown ornamental grasses, noted for its combination of size and open habit.

CLUMPS

The clump is the growth habit of a very large number of grass species, but here I wish to concentrate on those which form a relatively low clump. Such dumpy plants are quite the opposite of the graceful ones we have just considered, but this does not mean to say that they have no value in the garden. On the contrary, the garden needs large numbers of quietly attractive plants to give the star performers space and to let them be seen to best advantage. Many garden plants, particularly the more dramatic ones and the vast majority of later-flowering perennials, are upright growing in habit, and a lot of them tend to develop unattractive or bare stems at their bases. They need lower plants around them to hide their stems, cover the ground and fill in around them, especially at the front of the border.

In the wild, some clump-forming grasses form very large distinct tussocks, a nightmare to walk across. This natural look can be captured in the garden if tight clump-forming species are grown in proximity, and perhaps combined with naturally rounded hump-forming dwarf shrubs such as hebes and lavenders. Such shapes are not eye-catching but they have a pleasing harmonious quality.

Species of *Carex*, the sedges, include many of the best clump formers, with their tight masses of tidy leaves, very often interestingly covered. Most have arching leaves, which start off by growing upward and then radiate outward or arch over, effectively filling space at ground level, a habit often useful in containers or raised beds. Some, such as *Carex plantaginea*, have fewer, broader leaves which make a good contrast with other species. The woodrushes, species of *Luzula*, have a similar form to many of the *Carex* species and a slightly spreading habit that makes them good groundcover plants.

Grass clumps vary greatly in size: some species of *Festuca* form very small tufts, mainly worth growing for their distinctive colour. Plants with such a habit are useful for filling in among heathers, other dwarf shrubs and low-growing rockery-type plants. At the other end of the scale, *Cortaderia selloana* 'Aureolineata' forms really quite large clumps of distinctly yellow-lined leaves. They are big enough to be a valid part of shrub plantings and they offer a good contrast in form.

While it is the foliage of these plants that earns them a place in the garden, it is in fact the flowers that develop from some grasses, such as *Deschampsia*, that give them their unique character. Like many grasses, they produce multiple panicles comprising many spaced-out flowers/seed cases which form a softly textured cloud-like mass above and around the foliage, which is very useful for attractively filling in space at the front of the border around leggy late-flowering perennials.

OPPOSITE: The distinctive clumps of *Festuca mairei* form part of a dry landscape planting.

ABOVE: In mild areas *Stipa arundinacea* will stay green for much of the winter, gradually turning russet. Its form is always attractive.

LEFT: *Festuca amethystina*, normally blue-grey, takes on its autumn mode.

BELOW: The flower and seed heads of *Miscanthus* can provide six months of garden interest.

RIGHT: The neat habit of *Hakonechloa macra* allows the texture of the leaves to be enjoyed fully.

FAR RIGHT: The bamboo *Fargesia nitida* reveals its distinctive sheathed stems.

TEXTURE

Plants can look soft, such as a grass that forms a cloud-like head of masses of delicate flowers, or hard, such as one that has broad glossy leaves. Texture, like form, is one of those qualities that gives extra interest to a garden, and it is particularly useful at the end of the season or in winter, when there is not so much else to look at.

Texture also plays an important part in the way we look at a garden; soft-textured plants appear matt to the eye, absorbing light, which has the effect of making them recede, looking further away. Hard textures stand out; a glossy surface, or the pattern made by large or striking leaves, draws attention to itself, and thus appears closer than it really is. It thus stands to reason that a garden or border is going to look much smaller if a bold, especially a big and bold, plant is placed at the far end.

Plants form quite different patterns with their leaves. For example, *Luzula nivea* 'Marginata' forms rough rosettes of radiating broad leaves in contrast to its relative *L. nivea*, whose leaves are softer and narrower. Both make good groundcover in shade; the former looks quite striking, almost tropical in appearance, while the latter is more grass-like and consequently less striking, although for the brief period of its flowering season it makes far more impact with its soft creamy heads.

Some grasses tend to look a bit untidy after the wind has blown them about, whereas others maintain a remarkably well-tended look. A good example of the latter is *Hakonechloa macra*, whose leaves always look surprisingly tidy, as if the fairies come out and comb it every night, sweeping out from the centre of the clump.

The different textures bamboos develop is one of their distinguising characteristics. Those with small leaves, such as *Fargesia nitida*, look quite different from those like species of *Indocalamus*, which have much larger leaves, or those with long narrow leaves like *Pleioblastus linearis*. Species with leaves that hang right down to the ground, such as *Yushania anceps*, stand out too. Not everyone likes to mix bamboo species, but for those that do, juxtaposing these different textures is all part of the fun.

Bamboos are marvellous plants for looking at close up – the texture of the tall canes can be smooth and glossy, or covered in a hazy bloom. Some have glossier leaves than others, some have striations on the leaves, others not. The young emerging stems on mature plants in spring (known as culms) are also very attractive. It is these characteristics that make them such rewarding plants to have in a small space or somewhere where you frequently walk past them.

COLOUR

However attractive the forms and textures of so many grasses, I suspect that a large number of the people who have bought them for their gardens have done so for their foliage colour. For those unused to dealing with them, this is understandable. Most of us are more familiar with and thus more confident at dealing with colour in the garden than form, and it tends to be seen as a more important factor.

Grass foliage colours can never compete with flower colours, but why should they? Flower colours are so intense, compared to most foliage colours, that the eye can only take in so many of them. Most of us prefer flower colours to be in a certain proportion to less intense foliage colours; although lovers of massed ranks of bedding annuals will beg to differ. Green is, of course, the most important foliage colour, and one that is relaxing to look at, the perfect backdrop for flower colour. But some plants have brown, bronze or purple tones in their foliage, some even pink and red. Grasses and sedges are particularly strong on these colours. Silver, grey and blue foliage seem to enjoy periodic swings and falls in garden fashion, but always sell well in garden centres, whatever the current vogue. They provide variation, and look particularly effective with many flower colours. Finally, there are all those plants with variegated foliage, generally classified as having either white/cream/silver variegation or gold/yellow.

The great advantage of foliage colours over flowers is their much longer season, especially if they are evergreen. Flowers come and go, but foliage is there from spring to autumn at least, a boon in small gardens where every plant has to 'earn its keep'. Such a long season provides continuity, and can be used to establish a link from one season to the next. It is this long season, and the wide variety of colour, that has encouraged so many gardeners to turn to grasses.

TOP LEFT: *Achnatherum brachytricha* is an effective and relatively compact grass for late summer and autumn.

TOP CENTRE: *Chionochloa rubra* contrasts with the blue-grey foliage of *Cynara cardunculus*.

TOP RIGHT: *Milium effusum* 'Aureum' is known as Bowles' golden grass after the famous English gardener. It is useful for early summer colour, especially in light shade.

LEFT: Sunlight catches the variegated leaves of pampas grass *Cortaderia selloana* 'Silver Stripe'.

BELOW: *Deschampsia cespitosa* is a common plant of light woodland, which makes it eminently suitable for light shade in the garden.

RIGHT: The fresh green of the compact *Sesleria autumnalis* is useful for bordering paths.

FAR RIGHT: *Stipa arundinacea* is a superlative plant, with a long season of autumn colour.

GREENS

Green is such a dominant colour in the garden that it is rarely discussed. Yet there are so many different greens. I particularly like the fresh, slightly lemon green of *Melica altissima* 'Atropurpurea', which is one of those greens that looks fresh all the way through the year. Then there are the dark greens of *Deschampsia cespitosa* and of many bamboos. In between there are countless variations, many of which are only really appreciated when the plants are seen together.

When selecting plants or trying to place them in the garden, try to hold flowers against leaves and see which combinations look effective. Some greens definitely seem to intensify certain colours and dull others. A good example is the combination of scarlet with a clear mid-green, which seems to electrify both.

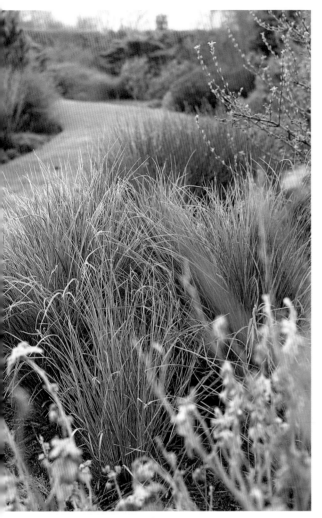

ADDING RED TO GREEN

Grasses and, perhaps even more, sedges are remarkable for the wide range of foliage colours that result from the addition of red to green: browns and bronzes. The most outstanding is the Japanese blood grass (*Imperata cylindrica*) with its wonderful red leaves, at their most dramatic when backlit. While there are no grasses yet available, commercially anyway, with purple foliage, there are plenty in the bronze to brown spectrum. These all look very attractive together, as the eye seems to appreciate a cavalcade of different and subtle variations on the same theme.

Of the bronze/brown leaved grasses, the finest, I think, is *Stipa arundinacea*, which has the added advantage of gradually developing its colours over time. During the growing season its arching leaves are dark olive green, turning golden-bronze in autumn, a tone that deepens through the winter, before dying to brown in the coldest weather. An evergreen, and less dynamic, version of these colours is offered by several New Zealand sedges that have recently become widely available; *Carex*

testacea and *C. dipsacea*, for example, have leaves that are a subtle blend of yellowy-greens and greeny-yellows, appreciated especially in the middle of winter.

Of the browns, the bronze form of *Carex comans* is often derided for looking dead. Yet no dead plant could have such a deep lustre to its fine bronze-brown leaves. But this colour is definitely one to be appreciated in context, to be a contrast to greens, or to be part of a spectrum of similar colours. It works well as a backdrop for yellow flowers; I grow it with late summer-flowering *Rudbeckia fulgida* var. *deamii*.

The great importance of the sedges is the opportunity they offer of using ever-greens in the border. Traditionally, evergreens have been limited to trees and shrubs, and borders have remained bare and brown through winter. Evergreen sedges in traditional dark green such as *Carex pendula* offer the opportunity to add this colour to the border for the winter, while the coloured-leaved species offer the more exciting possibility of dots and splashes of bronze and gold among the dormant perennials of winter. When spring starts, daffodils and narcissi find an echo of their flower colours among the colours of the sedges – this is important, as I find early spring bulbs seem to flower amid such bare surroundings, often lacking context for their flowers.

Given their ability to cope with poor soils and exposed conditions, perhaps the best use for all the bronze- and brown-leaved sedges is in combination with other plants that thrive is similar conditions: heathers, low-growing rhododendrons and dwarf conifers. Their colours mix well with the colours of heather and conifer foliage and they offer a striking contrast in form to the mound-forming heathers and spreading conifers.

ABOVE: Staying more or less the same colour all year round, the New Zealand sedge *Carex dipsacea* is another invaluable source of winter interest.

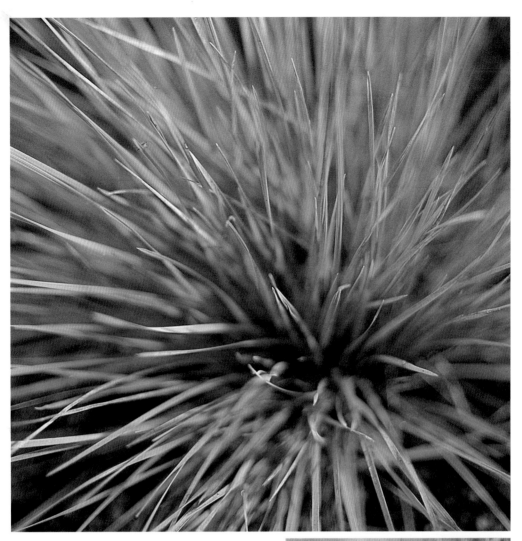

SILVER AND GREY

Some plants have a dense pattern of minute hairs on their leaves which gives them the appearance of having silver, grey or sometimes even blue-grey foliage. Most are from environments that regularly experience drought; the hairs help prevent water loss. They are of great value in the garden for the change they offer from green and the way they intensify colours such as pinks, blues and purples – in fact they work well with all colours except for yellows, which they tend to muddy. Grey and silver foliage mix well together too, making it possible to blend a variety of grassy and non-grassy species.

The deepest of these tones is that of *Elymus magellanicus*, which is definitely blue, but it can be short-lived, especially on moist soils. Other *Elymus* species are good, but tend to be invasive. Perhaps the best all-round medium silver grass is *Helictotrichon sempervirens*, which combines reliability with good colour. Plants of this size are effective as accent plants dotted around borders, and are useful for creating a sense of continuity and rhythm when

TOP: *Helictotrichon sempervirens* is one of the sources of the most reliable blue among grasses.

ABOVE: *Festuca amethystina* is one of many low-growing fescue grasses whose foliage offers the gardener a wide range of blue, grey and glaucous tones.

scattered in this way. They look good with grey-leaved plants from dry environments such as low- growing *Cistus*, *Perovskia* and lavender, their habit a contrast to the mound forms that so many dry climate or Mediterranean climate dwarf shrubs tend to take.

Large blue or grey grasses are rare, although a new variety, *Sorghastrum avenaceum* 'Sioux Blue' looks set to change this, as it grows to over a metre, and is thus potentially suitable for mixing with larger perennials. On a different scale are the silver-blue forms of *Festuca glauca*, of which several are now available. Their colour is good and they are easy to grow; they thrive on poor soils, making them useful companions for heathers and dwarf conifers. Their small size may appear to limit their usefulness, but not if they are used *en masse* as groundcover, where they are a very effective contrast to large plants like heathers. Their clump-forming habit does mean that there tend to be gaps between the plants, but I find this problem can be overcome if they are combined with species of *Acaena*, low-growing groundcover plants with tiny leaves in silver, grey and brown shades, or other similar rockery-type plants. The result is a ground-covering tapestry of subtly different shades. Such groundcover is effective alongside paving stones or filling the gaps between stepping stones.

TOP: *Elymus magellanicus* has the best blue of any grass. Although short-lived, it is easily raised from seed.

RIGHT: *Festuca* are tolerant of poor, sandy and limestone soils and exposure.

VARIEGATION

Variegation has long been prized in plants, partly for its novelty value, but mostly for the additional range of options it provides for creating plant compositions based on foliage colour. We have already seen how valuable grasses are that have leaves with colours other than green. The value of variegation, however, lies not just with leaf colour but with the pattern that the variegation takes; this may not be of great importance on the larger scale, but can be a factor that adds greatly to a plant's interest in small-scale or intimate schemes. The streaks and banding of silver or gold alongside the green of most variegated grasses is often worthy of this close attention. Sometimes, though, a

variation occurs which results in a grass having yellow-flushed foliage rather than true variegation. One such is *Milium effusum* 'Aureum', a species relatively tolerant of shade, where its light golden colour is especially welcome.

Most grasses with variegation are gold rather than silver, and most have it as an edging to the leaf. A form of pampas grass, *Cortaderia selloana* 'Aureolineata' is the largest of these. Its leaves are minutely edged with yellow, creating a neat mound of foliage that seems to glow soft gold, a very great improvement on the coarse leaves of the normal form. *Hakonechloa macra* 'Aureola' is another fine golden variegated grass, but it grows to only 30 centimetres. *Pleioblastus auricomus* is a golden bamboo. These truly golden species combine well with flowers in 'hot' colours while most other yellow variegated grasses tend to be paler, which makes them less outstanding in themselves but more suitable for combining with a wide variety of other colours.

TOP: Despite its aggressive growth, *Phalaris arundinacea* 'Feesey' is an attractive plant.

ABOVE: *Miscanthus sinensis* 'Strictus' is one of several cultivars with a unique pattern of variegation.

Cream variegation is perhaps the most common form among grasses; *Carex morrowii* 'Evergold' is one of the best, and it is useful for lightly shaded plantings and combining with low groundcover plants, especially those with broad foliage like bergenias and hostas. In contrast to the fine leaves of this species, *Carex siderosticha* 'Variegata' has very broad leaves, making it a good contrast to ferns.

White, rather than cream, variegation is, like the true gold, not so common. Clean white variegation is invaluable for mixing with strong colours, to calm them down and offer contrast. The finest is that of *Arundo donax* var. *versicolor*. It is not very hardy, but it is so beautiful and so exotic looking that it may be worth bringing under cover in winter; it looks stunning with dahlias and cannas in sub-tropical plantings. *Calamagrostis* x *acutiflora* 'Overdam' has white variegation and the splendidly upright habit of its parent *C.* x *acutiflora* 'Karl Foerster', making it useful for combining with lower-growing perennials with vivid flowers such as geranium or penstemon species.

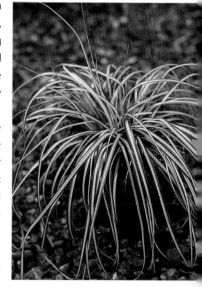

Nearly all grass variegation happens along the length of the leaf; in only a few very similar varieties does it occur across the leaf, to form bands: *Miscanthus sinensis* 'Zebrinus' and 'Strictus', for example. The plants are striking for their novelty value as well as being yellow enough to consort well with hot colours.

TOP LEFT: *Pleioblastus shibuyanus* 'Tsuboi' is a highly effective variegated bamboo. The dark green of *Indocalamus tessellatus* forms a strong contrast.

TOP RIGHT: Yellow-leaved *Milium effusum* 'Aureum' grows at the waterside.

ABOVE: *Carex morrowii* 'Evergold' makes a good container plant because of its tidy habit and evergreen foliage. It also thrives in light shade, so it is a versatile addition to a garden.

DRAMA

Plants can impress us through their colour, their form or through other qualities. Of these, drama is one of the most important to the gardener, and bamboos and grasses have plenty to offer here. But what makes a plant dramatic?

The unexpected is a major component: plants with very unusual foliage or shape that causes surprise when first seen. Size, too, often surprises: suddenly coming across a plant that is larger than one expects. We tend to think of grasses as being relatively small plants, so extra-large ones tend to stand out. Large foliage, whether it takes the form of very broad or very long leaves or tall stems, can surprise too, especially since it tends to be associated with tropical species, and can astonish when seen flourishing in a cooler climate. Foliage shape in itself can be a component of drama – leaf shapes that are unusual stand out as effectively and for the same reasons as unusual architecture or startlingly designed clothes.

Large grasses are some of the most important plants for the gardener who wants to introduce drama into the garden. They are a fantastic antidote to the twee cottagey style and safely soothing planting schemes that are so heavily promoted. Big, almost oversize, plants and striking leaves provide a feel that is contemporary and dashingly forward looking. US designer James van Sweden told me that 'small plants only make a small garden smaller' as he showed me his tiny back garden in downtown Washington DC, dominated by the huge sugar cane-like stems of *Miscanthus floridulus*.

The *Miscanthus* grasses include some of the most effectively dramatic grasses. It is not just the large size of some of them, but the elegant sweep of their seed heads above solid clumps of dark leaves that contribute to this quality. Other grasses create drama simply through sheer size, such as the grey-leaved but rather scruffy reed *Arundo donax*. This, and the larger species of *Miscanthus*, do best on moist soils, as do many plants with large foliage. They thrive with, and look remarkably good alongside, perennials with broad leaves like *Rheum* (ornamental rhubarb), *Rodgersia* and *Gunnera*. Combining such plants can create a very exotic impression; those gardeners who wish to conjure up the tropics or hint at the primeval should turn first to this plant selection.

Bamboos are also a good source of dramatic plants. Those that grow tall, such as *Semiarundinaria fastuosa*, are particularly striking, as are those that develop thick canes like *Phyllostachys violascens*. In Japan, bamboos with thick canes are frequently included in courtyard plantings, the canes rising out of gravel-covered earth, to grow upwards, often with their foliage up and out of sight, the whole presenting a planting dramatic in its simplicity but also hinting at a forest of tree trunks. Large-leaved bamboos, such as species of *Indocalamus* and *Susa*, are also particularly dramatic and exotic in effect.

ABOVE FAR LEFT: *Miscanthus sinensis* 'Strictus' is strongly banded.

ABOVE LEFT: *Miscanthus sinensis* 'Africa' is one of many dramatic varieties bred by German nurseryman Ernst Pagels.

FAR LEFT: *Miscanthus sinensis* 'Silberturm' is the tallest of the cultivars.

LEFT: *Miscanthus floridulus* is grown for its foliage rather than its flowers.

RIGHT: *Miscanthus sinensis* 'Ghana' is a new cultivar that acquires a rich autumn colouring.

ABOVE: Elegant flowers and habit and good autumn colour — *Miscanthus sinensis* 'Flamingo' is first class.

BELOW: *Calamagrostis* x *acutiflora* 'Karl Foerster', *Cortaderia selloana* and *Miscanthus sinensis* form the framework for a late summer border.

RIGHT: *Phyllostachys vivax* 'Aureocaulis' looks particularly poetic in the snow.

BELOW RIGHT: *Miscanthus sinensis* 'Pünktchen' combines variegated stripes with reliable autumn flowering.

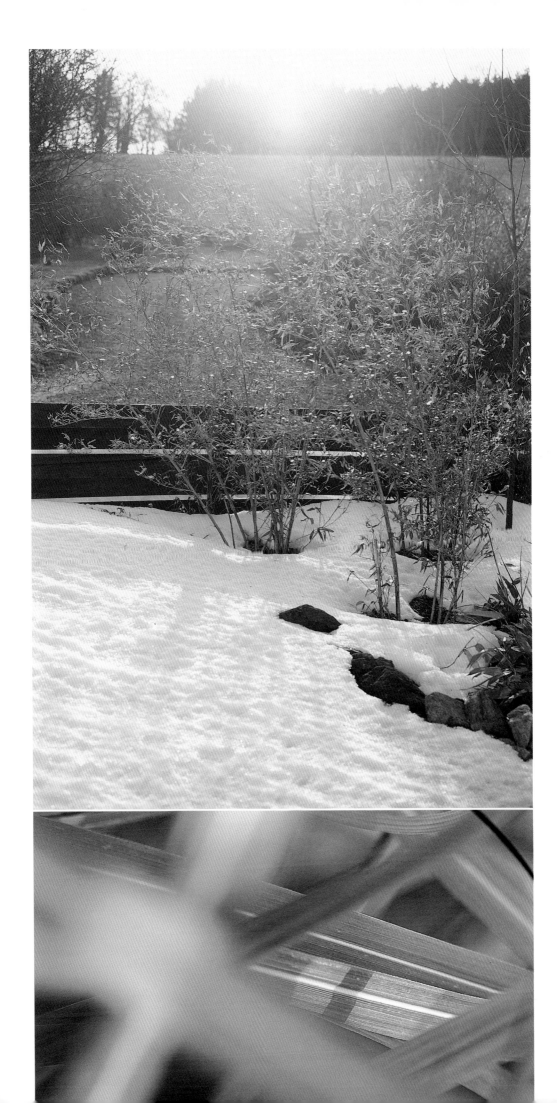

SOUND AND MOVEMENT

Walking through the countryside can be one of the best ways of appreciating some of the special features of grasses. Fields of long summer grass, or fields of wheat and barley, are in a state of constant movement in the slightest breeze; waves of motion cross the grass, as the flower heads bow to the wind and then spring back upright, before bowing again to the next gust. All the time there is the sound of wind swishing its way through the grass. Larger grasses, like fields of maize, bow less to the wind, but make more noise, as the large leaves rustle constantly against each other. Reed beds particularly are brought to life by the wind: the flower or seed heads all point in one direction, blown to one side by the prevailing wind, bending and bouncing back *en masse*. Their large and broad leaves make an especially distinctive sound.

Bamboos, with their large hard leaves and hollow stems, make a particularly dramatic sound as they move in the wind, the leaves slapping against each other, and the canes rattling. The larger the bamboo, the greater the sound. I shall never forget being in the mountain rain forest behind Rio de Janeiro beneath a vast bamboo in a storm. Huge canes banged into each other, others rubbed and scraped, making a sound that I can only liken to the creaking of a sailing ship, all against a backdrop of rustling leaves.

Nothing quite like this can be achieved in the temperate garden, but sound and movement are still features that give grasses a special place in the garden. Many grasses move in the slightest breeze, situations where other perennials stand stock still. Quaking grasses, the annual *Briza maxima* and the perennial *B.media*, with their

BELOW LEFT: Always in motion, the annual *Briza maxima* flowers only a few months from sowing seed.

BELOW RIGHT: The banding on yellow stems make *Phyllostachys aurea* 'Koi' a particularly fine form.

BELOW CENTRE RIGHT: A detail of a flower head of *Miscanthus sinensis* 'Ghana' shows its delicate feathering.

relatively heavy flower and seed heads hanging from light wiry stems, are particularly susceptible to air movement, as their common name indicates. Especially beautiful are those species, like *Miscanthus*, that have one-sided flower and seed heads, much like wild reeds; all bend to one side and move in unison as the wind blows through them. Plant them outlined against the sky, exposed to the wind, to appreciate their qualities.

Bamboos make good plants for courtyards and other confined spaces, partly because of their qualities of sound and movement. The absence of the sights and sounds of nature is one of the reasons why urban environments can be alienating to many people. Bamboos, with their response to the slightest breath of wind, are a very effective way of introducing such natural feelings and events into built-up places.

If these qualities appeal to you, then you could become a connoisseur of grass sounds. Each species really does make a different sound as it moves in the wind, depending on the size and number of leaves, and the height and distribution of the stems that carry the seed heads.

RIGHT: *Stipa gigantea* is nearly always in motion, as every breeze catches the flower heads.

BELOW RIGHT: *Miscanthus sinensis* 'Kaskade' — its name evokes the quantities of hanging flowers that this cultivar produces, which sometimes weigh down its stems.

CHANGE AND CONTINUITY

Nature is in a constant state of flux and change, or growth and death. For many people, this is an important part of the enjoyment of the garden, having spring flowers to look forward to, or autumn fruits. But it also creates certain problems: practical ones such as the need to clear away dead material and aesthetic ones such as the fact that there are times of the year when there is little to appreciate. It is not surprising that evergreens are popular – they provide continuity through the year, as well as always looking good. But the fact that they look pretty much the same, all year round, is a disadvantage; something that is always the same can be boring.

Grasses offer the gardener opportunities to explore change and continuity in ways that are highly advantageous. Grasses may flower, but their flowers are, in nearly all cases, pretty much identical to their seed heads, and most of us fail to notice when the former die and turn into the latter. Conventional flowers can be nine-day wonders, but this is not the case with grasses: their flower/seed head interest often lasting for months. Perhaps the briefest period of interest is that of *Luzula nivea*, with about ten days of cream flowers in early summer, or *Melica altissima* 'Atropurpurea', which has wonderful dark purple flowers a little later, but whose colour is lost after the flowers die. Many though flower in summer, develop seed heads, and are still hanging on looking reasonably attractive in late winter, such as the plume-like heads of many *Miscanthus*. *Calamagrostis* x *acutiflora* 'Karl Foerster' has perhaps the longest season; flowering in early summer, its seed heads still make a dramatic feature in the garden next spring.

While evergreens provide the most obvious sense of continuity in the garden, the long season of many grasses contributes continuity too, but one that also includes a feeling for the natural rhythm of the seasons. The interesting and rather convenient thing for us, is how effectively grasses complement flowers in the garden, often looking their best when flowers have the least to offer. Spring is when we are least likely to appreciate grasses, although the fresh green growth of some is a welcome addition to the garden. Some of the best ornamental grasses though are among the very last garden plants to start into growth; *Miscanthus* and *Panicum* do not really start moving until spring has almost turned into summer.

Early summer, the time when so many perennials and roses are looking their best, sees quite a few grasses come into their own, generally the more quietly beautiful ones. The yellow-flushed leaves of *Milium effusum* 'Aureum'

ABOVE RIGHT: *Melica macra* is the showiest of this delicate-looking genus, but looks good for only a short time.

RIGHT: *Miscanthus sinensis* 'Malepartus' is one of the best of the larger *M. sinensis* cultivars; this one looks particularly fine in autumn.

ABOVE FAR RIGHT: Even in spring, the dried leaves of *Miscanthus* remaining from the previous year's growth can be attractive.

FAR RIGHT: A *Miscanthus* with *Eupatorium maculatum* 'Atropurpureum' in the background: a classic late summer combination for the larger border.

complement purple ornamental garlic flowers perfectly, or in shadier spots the blue flowers of the comfrey *Symphytum caucasicum*. The relatively shade-tolerant *Melica* grasses also look their best now, their delicate flowers nodding above broad fresh green leaves. On the whole, though, the role of grasses at this time is strictly to be a complement to the flowers, those with coloured foliage, such as silver-leaved *Elymus* and *Helictotrichon*, being the most useful alongside the numerous pastel shades of this season.

Late summer and early autumn sees grasses play a more important role, but still it is a largely complementary one. Summer-flowering species like *Miscanthus* and *Molinia* stand among the profusion of perennials that flower at this time, offering qualities of form and texture alongside the rich flower colours, and perhaps offer some rest and respite to the eye. Some of these late flowers are very large, like the *Miscanthus*, and perform alongside the perennials at their own level. Given that so many late perennials are tall and somewhat leggy, it is useful to be able to include lower-growing grasses, like varieties of *Deschampsia* with their cloud-like seed heads or the oat-like *Chasmanthium latifolium* (syn. *Uniola latifolia*) at the front of the border.

ABOVE LEFT: The attractive seed heads of *Molinia caerulea* ssp. *arundinacea* are immensely fine.

ABOVE RIGHT: In late autumn, the delicate seed heads of *Molinia caerulea* 'Fontäne' look stunning.

BELOW: *Calamagrostis* x *acutiflora* 'Karl Foerster' (left) with *Stipa gigantea* stand out in the border at the very end of the growing season.

It is in late autumn and winter that grasses really come into their own. While a few collapse at the end of the season (notably several *Molinia*) the majority stand up to the weather remarkably well. By the time the last of the year's flowers have died, the grasses are arguably looking their best. It is not just the wide variety of seed heads but the subtle tones of dead leaves and stems, as soft winter light illuminates a wide variety of tones of fawn and brown. The low, almost sideways, direction of winter sunlight is particularly effective at making the most of these, as it is at catching the silvery seed heads of *Cortaderia* and *Miscanthus*. Leaving the dead stems of grasses and perennials standing provides infinitely more interest in the garden in winter than cutting them all down, as many gardeners have done up to now. Birds find not only the seeds to eat, but a host of insect larvae hidden in old seed heads. It is not generally until late in the winter that the old growth begins to look so untidy that it reaches the stage when it needs to be cleared away.

Winter weather such as snow and particularly hoarfrost can add a further dimension to grasses. Snow will dramatically emphasize anything still standing, such as the taller grasses or the foliage of bamboos, each leaf supporting a narrow strip of snow. Hoarfrost coats a thin layer of ice crystals along every available edge of leaf, stem and seed head, highlighting details like nothing else does.

ABOVE LEFT: *Cortaderia selloana* 'Silver Stripe' is one of the lower-growing variegated pampas grasses.

ABOVE RIGHT: The late summer evening sun emphasizes the tall canes of (from left to right) *Phyllostachys aurea* 'Holochrysa', *P. aurea* and *P.a.* 'Koi'.

THE KEY TO USING GRASSES IN
THE GARDEN IS MATCHING THE
ENVIRONMENT TO THE PLANT,
BOTH IN PHYSICAL AND VISUAL
TERMS. HERE WE LOOK AT A
VARIETY OF WAYS GRASSES CAN
BE USED, SO THE ESSENTIAL
CHARACTERISTICS OF EACH ARE
DISPLAYED TO THEIR BEST
ADVANTAGE AND DIFFERENT
ENVIRONMENTS ARE ENHANCED
BY THE SPECIES SELECTED.

IN YOUR GARDEN

OPPOSITE: Bamboo is an essential part of any Far Eastern-style garden. This is
Pleioblastus shibuyanus 'Tsuboi'.

ABOVE: The massive canes of bamboo *Phyllostachys viridiglaucescens* tower skywards.

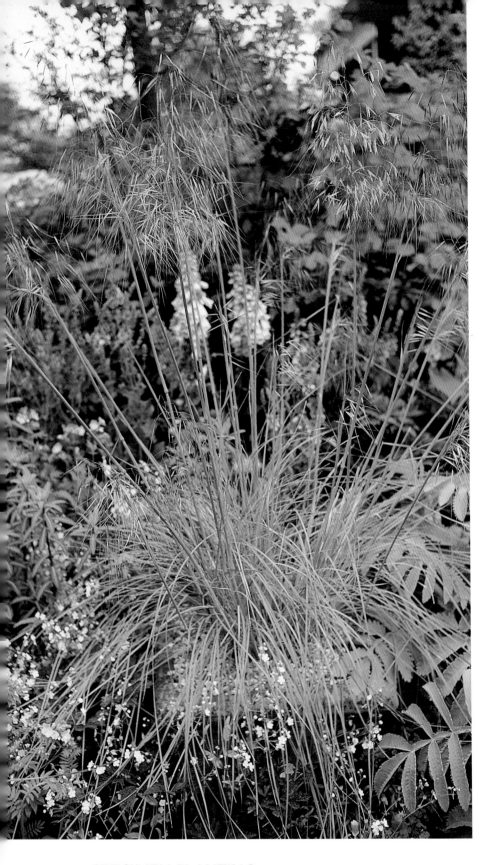

SPECIMEN PLANTING

A specimen plant is one that is grown on its own, in splendid isolation, surrounded by grass or other groundcover, as is the case with a single tree in a lawn. It is the best way to show off a plant whose distinct character is best appreciated when it is grown uncluttered by neighbours. Specimen plants need to look good all over for as much of the year as possible; species that have features that need hiding do not make good specimens. On a smaller scale, the term can also be used to describe plants grown as individuals in containers, which is the most effective way of creating a specimen plant in a small area, rather like putting it on a pedestal. Many of the neat, coloured-leaf sedges, such as *Carex testacea*, can look good grown in this way.

Pampas grass, *Cortaderia selloana*, is the classic specimen grass, but unfortunately it has been so widely planted in places that are simply too cramped for it, that it has become something of a cliché of suburbia: usually seen planted dead centre in the front lawn of a bungalow by someone with delusions of grandeur. The best planting of it I

LEFT: The well-proportioned shape of *Stipa gigantea* lends itself to specimen planting, so that its elegance can be appreciated. Here it is planted in a container.

BELOW: Many bamboos are best appreciated as specimen plants surrounded by grass. This is *Fargesia robusta*.

LEFT: Chilean *Chusquea culeou* has a dense clump-forming habit, making it ideal for specimen planting.

OPPOSITE BELOW LEFT: The linear foliage of a potted *Fargesia murieliae* is contrasted with the naturally rounded forms of pebbles used to line the container.

OPPOSITE BELOW RIGHT: The tangled form of a *Carex* species along with *Pennisetum orientale* makes an effective container-planting combination.

BELOW LEFT: The broad leaves of *Indocalamus latifolius* makes it a good species for specimen planting.

BELOW RIGHT: Woodrush *Luzula nivea* is reasonably tolerant of dry shade, making it a potentially very useful plant, especially for the difficult planting conditions found under trees.

have ever seen was the use of several clumps together in a loose group in a vast expanse of lawn. Perhaps it is best used as a border plant in most of our gardens, rather than trying and failing to make a good specimen planting of it!

Miscanthus sinensis is an elegant version of pampas grass. Although deciduous, it makes a fine specimen in lawn after a couple of years – it forms a neat clump and its seed heads form magnificent plumes atop tall stems. There are many varieties in a good range of sizes. Another grass that begs to be grown in this way is *Stipa gigantea*, whose bunches of oat-like seed heads hang from long stems flung in all directions; it should be grown in plenty of space to display its characteristic form at its best.

If there is a big enough area of lawn and the site not too exposed or dry, bamboos make superb specimen plants. Only those that form tight clumps and do not run are suitable, with those that grow upright and arch at the top most attractive. Species of *Chusquea*, *Fargesia* and *Thamnocalamus* are suitable, the latter useful for soils that do not remain moist in summer. Black-stemmed *Phyllostachys nigra* can be used as well.

GRASSES IN BORDERS

GRASSES AND BORDER STYLES

Borders provide homes for the majority of the plants we grow in our gardens. Originally a border was literally that – a strip along a backdrop such as a fence, wall or hedge; the form developed to its climax in Edwardian Britain with grand herbaceous borders, using only perennials, and mostly late-flowering ones. Since then, the mixed border has become more commonplace, comprising shrubs and annuals alongside perennials. The 1960s saw the development of 'island beds', self-contained groups of shrubs and perennials surrounded by lawn or paving, very different from the traditional border, as there was no backdrop. Some garden designers experimented with other forms of planting that also did without a backdrop, inspired in Britain by the traditional cottage garden, in Germany by natural wildflower meadows, and in the US by the prairie.

The various different forms that borders take have implications for what kind of plants work best in them. The traditional border, where there is a backdrop, and which is appreciated from one side only, works very well for plants that can look scruffy after flowering, or have long bare stems – all of which can be effectively hidden by having other plants grow in front of them to an appropriate height. It also works well for flowers, because the vast majority are highlighted by being seen against a background. But many grasses are arguably not particularly well served by this kind of border; their distinct form is liable to be buried or obscured by surrounding foliage, and there is not enough space to appreciate the patterns created by the radiating flower stems of those like *Stipa gigantea* or *Molinia*. Upright-growing species with fine seed heads like *Calamagrostis* or many species of *Stipa* are only seen to best advantage against the sky. Even in island beds, they can seem hemmed in. It is not surprising that it is the nature-inspired open border styles that were developed by German and US designers that use grasses most extensively and effectively.

BELOW: A border on moist soil in early summer: *Carex elata* 'Aurea' is in the centre, with *Molinia caerulea* 'Variegata' to the right. The large grass at the far right is a *Cortaderia*.

ABOVE RIGHT: A variety of grasses — including (from left) *Deschampsia cespitosa* 'Goldtau', *Achnatherum brachytrichum*, *Hakonechloa macra* and the leafy green *Stipa calamagrostis* — transform a border designed by Piet Oudolf in late summer. The prominent red perennial is *Persicaria amplexicaule* 'Firetail'.

USING DENSE LOW-GROWING GRASSES

Rounded clump-like grasses, especially those with coloured foliage, can, however, work well in conventional borders with a backdrop, or in the cottage-garden style, where the juxtaposition of individual plants is very important. They can be very effective used either in blocks comprising several individuals of the same variety, where they will make a real, if unsubtle, impact, or dotted throughout a planting to create a sense of rhythm, so that the same plant (with its most usefully long season of interest) is repeated at either regular, or random but evenly spaced, intervals. Such repeated dotting of the same plant can create a powerful sense of visual unity in a border, or even in the whole garden, with a strong sense of seasonal continuity as well.

Small dense grasses are particularly useful in confined spaces. A coloured-leaf sedge, one of the *Carex* species, can provide variety of colour among a small group of low-growing perennials, while the delicate sprays of fine flower heads of *Deschampsia* can complement the broad leaves of a hosta or the rosettes of fern foliage.

Modern low-maintenance plantings can make great use of low coloured-leaf grasses when they are used in blocks, alternating with low-growing shrubs like heather and dwarf conifers in exposed situations, or with grey-leaved plants like lavenders, sages and *Cistus*, or rock rose, in hot drought-prone ones. Given their small size, they can be used to create flexible and fluid patterns around the larger plants.

USING SMALL LIGHT AIRY GRASSES

These are the grasses that are really likely to get lost, that have to be observed close up to appreciate their sometimes elfin beauty. They should never be planted where they can be obscured by their neighbours, and often look best when there is a whole mass of them together; a patch of any of the *Melica* species in dappled shade, for example, is a lovely and arresting sight – whereas one on its own would probably not even be noticed. Fortunately, most grow easily enough from seed, so it is possible to start from one plant and have many more to plant out within the year.

USING LARGER LIGHT AIRY GRASSES

Big enough to stand on their own, but needing space to be properly appreciated, grasses like *Stipa gigantea* and *Molinia* look their best in modern open-border style plantings, surrounded by low-growing perennials like *Sedum spectabile* or *Rudbeckia fulgida* var. *deamii*; dwarf shrubs like *Thymus* or other, much lower grasses. Most gardens will accommodate only one of these magnificent plants; larger areas can be planted with a widely spaced group of them. They look best with sky behind them, or planted on a slope so their stems hang out into the space above plants growing at a lower level.

Airy grasses that have a rather less distinctive habit – more conventionally upright perhaps, like *Stipa capillata* or *Panicum virgatum* – can be combined much more easily with perennials their own size, but they should not be hemmed in. They can look especially good grown *en masse*, but mixed with flowering perennials of a similar light and airy growth habit, such as *Aster lateriflorus*. A small open area can thus conjure up the feeling of a wild meadow.

ABOVE LEFT: The prairie grass *Sporobolus heterolepis* looks especially wonderful when covered in morning dew.

ABOVE RIGHT: The *Miscanthus* species combine bulk and majesty with delicacy and elegance. *Miscanthus sinensis* 'Africa' is a new variety.

RIGHT: *Molinia caerulea* subsp. *arundinacea* is a wonderfully delicate tall species for the late summer or autumn border.

USING LARGER UPRIGHT GRASSES

Larger grasses have plenty of presence; whether used singly, widely spaced or *en masse* is a matter of taste. Very upright *Calamagrostis* x *acutiflora* 'Karl Foerster' is stunning in a loose group surrounded by lower-growing perennials or dwarf shrubs like heathers, but can be lost among taller plants. In a dense clump in a modern open garden, they lose some of their individual character but gain something else as a group, a hint of the prairie or a reed bed.

Those grasses, like the *Miscanthus*, that bear distinctive flower and seed heads are among the most flexible. They create the impression of a reed bed if grown in groups in an open site, but look equally good in a traditional border setting – their plumes rise above the level of most perennials and they look good against solid backdrops as well as sky. To appreciate them in winter, let the sun strike them sideways or backlight them.

USING BAMBOOS

Bamboos have a shrub-like bulk, are evergreen, but have infinitely more elegance than the vast majority of shrubs. Potentially, they are very useful in mixed borders as shrub substitutes, but their need for shelter from wind and hot sun and for a moist soil may limit their use. Some, like *Indocalamus* species, whose main interest lies in their large and distinctive foliage, can be combined easily with a wide variety of plants, whereas many of the others need to be positioned so their style is not cramped; we need to be able to see the whole length of the canes of many and the graceful arching of the upper parts of their stems. Those that run, needless to say, should only be included in the border if they are enclosed in something like a bottomless flower pot or sheets of slate.

ABOVE LEFT: *Melica ciliata* is a relatively small species that adds a touch of the natural landscape to garden plantings.

ABOVE RIGHT: *Panicum virgatum* is inconspicuous until it flowers in late summer.

BELOW: The variegation of *Pleioblastus variegatus* echoes the flowers of an *Azalea*.

RIGHT: *Miscanthus sinensis* 'Flamingo' (rear) combines with *Stipa calamagrostis*.

FAR RIGHT: The tall skyward-pointing plumes of *Cortaderia selloana* 'Silver Fountain' needs plenty of space around it to be appreciated at its best.

USING GRASSES WITH PERENNIALS

Grasses are the natural accompaniment to perennials: after all, most of the sun-loving perennials we grow in our gardens grow naturally as wildflowers in meadows and prairies, habitats that are dominated by grasses. The addition of grasses to a border helps to make the planting look wilder and closer to nature and the soft textures of the grasses are the perfect complement to the shapes and the colours of many flowers.

Garden perennials can be roughly divided into two groups: those that are identical to, or at least close to, their wild ancestors and maintain the proportions, if not the colours, of their forebears, so they are still immediately recognizable as members of the same family; and those that have been intensively hybridized and demonstrate it, having lost the elegant natural proportions of wildflowers. Examples of the latter include many of the delphinium and lupin hybrids, asters, chrysanthemums and hemerocallis. They look out of place in any situation that is not obviously a garden, and simply do not combine well with grasses. The former, though, almost always look good alongside grasses.

Gardeners have been very selective, perhaps too selective, in choosing wildflowers to grow as garden plants. Recently, however, there has been much experimentation with using a much wider range of wild plants in the border. One garden designer who is at the forefront of working with both grasses and wild perennials newly introduced to cultivation is Piet Oudolf in the Netherlands. He is particularly fond of using plants that belong to the umbellifer family (the cow parsley, hogweed and angelica group) – never colourful in the conventional sense but which have elegance, delicacy and sometimes magnificence. Many of these plants are, like grasses, major components of woodland-edge ior natural meadow habitats. Combined with other traditionally used perennials and grasses they can be used to create the most wonderfully naturalistic schemes.

USING GRASSES WITH SHRUBS

Shrubs occupy a great deal of space in gardens, and when not in flower they can be dull and visually domineering. The late season of grasses makes them potentially good companions, although varieties should be carefully selected. Light and airy species tend not to combine well; those with more bulk such as *Miscanthus* hold their own better visually, while low-growing clump-forming species can be used at the base of the shrub canopy to provide interest at ground level. Shrubs with dark foliage, such as hollies, can be a good backdrop for those with light-coloured seed heads or pale foliage, like *Calamagrostis* x *acutiflora* 'Overdam'. If conditions are suitable, bamboos mix with shrubs on their own terms in size and scale; their elegant shapes very effective next to more amorphous shrub shapes.

Given that shrubs can cast shade and they tend to extract considerable quantities of moisture and nutrients from the soil, you should ensure that conditions are suitable for grasses before planting around established shrubs. Soil that is full of roots is unlikely to be suitable. Conversely, grasses grow more rapidly than young shrubs, and they should not be planted within 80 centimetres of newly planted stock.

USING GRASSES WITH BULBS

Most bulbs and grasses look their best at opposite times of the year to each other. By careful organization a succession of interest can be arranged, so that bulbs are planted around the base of late-flowering late-emerging grasses like *Miscanthus* and *Panicum*. By the time the grasses begin to grow in late spring, crocus and snowdrops (*Galanthus*) are dormant, and most daffodils and narcissi are nearly so. In the autumn, the grasses are at their peak, filling the space that the bulbs take up in the spring.

USING GRASSES WITH ANNUALS

The quickest grasses to establish are those annual species that can be sown in the ground to flower only a few months later, such as the fluffy hare's tail, *Lagurus ovatus,* or the quaking grass, *Briza maxima*. They make excellent companions for pretty cottage garden-type annuals like love-in-a-mist (*Nigella*), English marigolds (*Calendula officinalis*) or any of the new generation of natural-looking annuals and half-hardy perennials. As with perennials, annuals should be chosen for their wild looks, not the top-heavy highly bred French marigolds (*Tagetes*) or petunias.

EXPOSED AND DIFFICULT CONDITIONS

Grasses are some of the most useful of all plants for those gardens that experience the
worst of what the elements can throw at them; wind, salt spray, cold or drought. The
right species do have to be chosen, but it is true to say that grasses are among the most
tolerant of all garden plants, and there are some exceptionally good plants for the
most testing conditions. Quite apart from their tolerance, the structure of grasses
seems almost specifically designed for exposed and other difficult places: there are no
boughs or delicate flower stems to break; they bend in the wind to bounce back up
again once the tempest subsides; and their growth points are protected by nearly
always being at, or near, the base of the plant at ground level, so that if the leaves are
broken or eaten, more can be rapidly and plentifully produced.

Cold exposed gardens are ideal for a number of grasses from heathland habitats,
including true grasses like *Molinia caerulea*, and many sedges, including the coloured-
leaved New Zealand species like *Carex testacea*. The fact that the latter are evergreen
is a terrific boon in situations that can be extremely bleak in winter.

Warmer, but still exposed, gardens are suitable for practically all grasses, with many
withstanding hurricane-force winds. Many grasses also survive in coastal gardens that
experience winds that are laden with salt, which can do terrific damage to many foliage
plants. Those most suitable are those with a grey or blue tinge to their foliage, such as
the blue oat grass, *Helictotrichon sempervirens*, or species of wild rye grass, or *Elymus*;
the colour indicating the tiny hairs that protect against sun scorch, desiccation and salt
spray. Indeed many species of *Elymus* are originally from maritime environments. The
grey tones of the foliage often seem appropriate to coast settings as well, as does the
upright character of the foliage, which forms a contrast to flat horizons.

FAR LEFT: The rich brown foliage of clumps of evergreen *Carex buchananii* is the perfect complement to exposed and weathered stonework in the winter garden.

CENTRE LEFT: *Festuca amethystina* takes on glorious colour in the autumn. It is one of many fescues that are ideal for exposed conditions.

CENTRE RIGHT: *Helictotrichon sempervirens*, the blue oat grass, like many other blue-grey grasses, survives dry conditions well, which makes it extremely useful.

RIGHT: *Leymus arenarius*, an exquisitely blue species, looks especially good in spring, when the new leaves at at their freshest and the colour is most intense.

Many grasses are also suitable for gardens that are drought prone, although careful selection of species will have to be made. Again, those with grey foliage are usually good, as well as any plants known to come from areas of steppe, extensive areas of grassy plains, or areas of semi-desert, such as most of the *Stipa* grasses, or from dry prairies, such as the big bluestem, *Andropogon gerardii*. Apart from those species known to be moisture-lovers, most of the grasses are reasonably drought tolerant. Moreover, they usually do not look quite as dreadful as perennials and shrubs can after an extended period of drought, and they often recover faster.

One characteristic of many perennials and shrubs from difficult environments is that they have a spectacular but brief period of flowering; think of the brilliant splashes of colour on Mediterranean hillsides in spring, and moorland hills ablaze with purple heather in summer. Grasses, the evergreen ones especially, help to even out this rather unbalanced flowering pattern through the year, providing interest in every season. They also look attractive and appropriate planted alongside the characteristic hummocky shapes of dwarf shrubs such as lavender and heather that tend to be the planting mainstay of such difficult situations.

WATER GARDENS

An essential part of many natural waterside environments is the presence of grasses, such as reed beds fringing lakes and tough clumps of rushes next to mountain streams.Grasses can do much to enhance water features in the garden also, particularly in blurring the edges between the water itself and the rest of the garden. Such a blurring creates the impression that the body of water is natural. Even if it is intentionally not natural, and very formal in design, the soft textures of grasses and their shapes usually complement the clear horizontals of water and edging. Having plants that arch out over water is an effect that can be especially pleasing; many grasses are valuable here, such as the catkin-like flower and seed heads of the sedge *Carex pendula*, arching out on wiry stems.

In discussing appropriate grasses for gardens, the distinction must be made between moisture-loving species and those that need or tolerate ordinary garden soils, but which look like waterside grasses. Moisture-loving species of the true grasses are nearly always vigorous growers with a spreading, often aggressive, habit, making it essential that varieties are chosen appropriate to the size of the water feature. Many

OPPOSITE ABOVE: Cotton grass, *Eriophorum angustifolium*, is a plant for acid soils.

OPPOSITE BELOW: *Carex elata* 'Aurea' adds a sparkle to the waterside.

ABOVE: *Miscanthus* are good near water as they evoke the look of wild reeds without their invasive habits.

ABOVE TOP RIGHT: Grasses and water go together naturally — this is made the most of in this garden.

ABOVE RIGHT: A selection of bamboos, some clipped to make a hedge Japanese style, surround a pond.

BELOW: *Molinia caerulea* subsp. *arundinacea* is a taller, more upright form of the robust purple moor grass.

waterside sedges are competitive runners too. Given that many familiar waterside grasses are so competitive, it is fortunate that there are smaller versions available of some of them; the distinctive reed maces for example (*Typha* species) are suitable for only the largest ponds, yet there is a dwarf form – *Typha shuttleworthii*.

Creation of a successful natural-style water garden involves the development of a moisture gradient that runs from the water through the water margin to waterlogged soil, moist soil and finally dry land. Such a gradient offers a wide range of habitats for plants and for the wildlife that is such an essential feature of a natural pond. Some grasses can be grown in the water itself as marginal plants, such as *Carex elata* 'Aurea' or species of *Scirpus* and *Typha*. Others are happier in wet ground on the bank, such as *Phalaris arundinacea*. Then there are those that do best in constantly moist, but not sodden, soil, like *Molinia*. Many of the latter do as well in ordinary garden conditions, making them useful for a situation that often occurs: the water is enclosed in a liner that does not allow for gradation from water to dry land. Marginals in pots may be sunk into the water's edge, but there is no wet ground. *Miscanthus*, which look like refined reeds, are ideal for planting next to water, to create the impression of natural marshland.

WILD GARDENS

A key and very obvious distinction between wild plant communities and the garden is the predominance of grasses in so many open habitats, and their almost total absence in the vast majority of gardens, except as lawn, kept obsessively mown. It is not surprising that the development of a more natural garden style has gone hand in hand with an increase in the appreciation of grasses, and the linking of natural inspiration to gardens and landscapes by designers such as James van Sweden in the US, Piet Oudolf in the Netherlands and Urs Walser in Germany. Starting with the lawn, why not let it grow a little, to encourage low-growing wildflowers like daisies and cowslips? Many gardeners have taken this a stage further, by trying to establish wildflower meadows as alternatives to lawns. Unfortunately the majority of attractive meadow wildflowers are natives of thin European grassland, and are rapidly swamped by grasses on the majority of soils. Even if slow-growing, non-competitive grasses are used, aggressive species often seed themselves naturally after a number of years, and on most soils then take over. However, for thin soils, or a substrate of sand or crushed rubble, they, and their accompanying limestone flora grasses, are immensely suitable. Some of the grasses are quite beautiful in themselves, such as the perennial quaking grass, *Briza media*.

On most soils of average fertility and moisture content, where it is difficult to establish meadow wildflowers, simply letting coarse lawn grass grow can result in areas of long grass of great beauty. Such areas can be made to look intentional, rather than just neglected, if paths of mown grass are made through them, or cut around them, or their context is a relatively formal one.

Regions of clearly defined continental climates are most suitable for prairie-style plantings; clump-forming grasses such as species of *Andropogon* are used as a matrix for tall late-flowering perennials. Natural prairie has a highly fertile soil and a flora of incredible richness and diversity. Prairie restoration is becoming very popular as a garden and land-scape style in the Midwest of the United States: it is good for wildlife and needs far less water than conventional planting or lawn grass.

Borders can be made to look more natural by using grasses, almost any grasses, that contribute an air of natural insouciance, especially those with prominent flowers or seed heads. The use of multiples of one or two varieties of grass scattered throughout a planting is particularly effective at hinting at meadow or prairie, with their natural close association of perennials and grasses.

The most effective grasses at developing a natural feel are those that look as if they could be superior natives of the area, rather than the exotic looking, or obviously unnatural, like variegated varieties. Species of *Calamagrostis*, *Stipa* and *Pennisetum* are highly attractive and fit easily into a wide variety of landscapes.

LEFT: *Melica transsilvanica* grows alongside magenta *Geranium sanguineum* and other drought-tolerant wild plants.

ABOVE: The extraordinarily long awns of *Stipa pulcherrima* wave in the breeze among a selection of steppe (dry grassland) species.

OPPOSITE: Wild grasses evoke a sense of romance, though some regard them as untidy.

BELOW LEFT: *Holcus mollis* 'Albovariegatus' looks especially bright in spring.

BELOW RIGHT: Clumps of *Carex elata* 'Aurea' are used to edge a path.

BOTTOM LEFT: *Koeleria*, though not a runner, makes effective groundcover for shade.

BOTTOM RIGHT: The quaking grass, *Briza media*, can be used in meadows on drier soils.

FAR RIGHT: *Luzula sylvatica* is an excellent evergreen groundcover plant for difficult shade.

GROUNDCOVER

Lawns are the obvious and most common use of plants as groundcover; planting which is functional as much as it is decorative, aiming to please as an overall impression rather than with detail. Alternatives to grass as groundcover have traditionally been used only in areas where lawn grass will not grow – chiefly the use of reliable evergreens such as ivy in shade. The varieties chosen have tended to be dark green, dull, and to have given the concept of groundcover rather a bad name in some quarters. Recently, more adventurous use of groundcover plants, mainly in the US, has encouraged a more positive outlook. So what is grass as a groundcover if it is not lawn?

Lawn is maintained at an artificially low height by mowing, whereas groundcover grasses are allowed to grow to their normal height, which is usually fairly low. Ground-cover in shade tends to be functional, but it can be decorative: woodrushes (*Luzula* species) are spreading evergreens tolerant of dry shade, and they are moderately attractive. The more lush and attractive *Carex muskingumensis* is one of several suitable species of sedges that thrive in damp shade. The most elegant of shade groundcovers for light shade are the *Melica* grasses, which can form a lawn-like growth to a height of around 30 centimetres when flowering. Their impression is one of great delicacy,but the *Melicas* do not spread like lawn grasses or many sedges. Large numbers of plants would need to be raised from seed to create much of a spectacle.

Groundcover in sun tends to be chosen on more positive grounds than that in the shade. Low-growing grasses like the blue-green varieties of *Festuca glauca* have been the most commonly used till now, but there is no reason why taller species should not be used, perhaps putting the running habit of *Leymus arenarius* to good use, for example. Species of *Pennisetum* are used extensively as groundcover, their fluffy flower/seed heads tending to flop slightly and mesh together by late summer, to make up for the fact their clumps of leaves do not. However, they are only reliable as groundcover for areas with a continental climate.

As an alternative to the greyish tones predominating among many of the sun-loving grasses that are suitable for use as groundcover, the warm browns of the New Zealand sedges should be considered. Low-growing and brown *Carex comans* is the most suitable but others are worth looking at. When planning groundcover, it is worth considering whether you want a uniform look, with solid blocks of multiples of the same variety of grass, or a more naturalistic blending of different varieties. Both can be highly effective ways of contrasting different foliage colours, forms and textures, the former looking more appropriate in urban surroundings, the latter in rural ones. The blended approach only really works if plants of roughly similar height are chosen, whereas if block planting is done, contrasts in height between different blocks can be part of the overall effect.

ABOVE: *Festuca glauca* makes a strong contrast to the purple foliage of the Japanese maple, *Acer palmatum* 'Atropurpureum'.

RIGHT: *Shibataea kumasasa* is a very effective dwarf bushy bamboo for small spaces.

CENTRE RIGHT: The bolder gardener should consider how effective large grasses such as *Miscanthus sinensis* 'Ghana' can be in small gardens.

FAR RIGHT: Bamboos are surprisingly effective in confined as well as large areas, as this *Thamnocalamus tessellatus* and *Chimonobambusa marmorea* demonstrate.

SMALL SPACES

Small spaces in gardens are difficult because every plant tends to be on view the whole time; there is no room for anything that looks tatty for very long. Plants with a long season, such as grasses, are inherently more suitable than short-lived wonders, however spectacular. Confined areas can also be difficult because the prevailing conditions are often somewhat unfriendly to many plants: shade or hot sun, depending on the aspect of walls; draughts and gusts of wind tearing around corners, rubble-filled beds at the foot of foundations. Grasses, with the exception of bamboos, are well suited to many trying conditions, which makes them even more suitable for such places.

Views on planting small places differ. I share the opinion of those like designer James van Sweden (*see page* 37), that small places need dignifying and magnifying through the use of large plants; big *Miscanthus* and bamboos. But there are those, especially those who love collecting plants for their own sake, that favour the use of a larger variety of small ones. It all comes down to personal taste.

Traditional Japanese courtyards often feature bamboos, and where there is shade and a reasonably moist soil, or the certainty of being able to keep them watered, they make some of the finest plants for confined places. The height of many varieties can create the impression of being in a forest. Others are useful for the fact that, unlike woody shrubs, they are inclined to be tall and thin and thus fit into tight spaces better. There are also attractively bushy miniature species like *Shibataea kumasasa*.

Grasses with details that go unnoticed in the wider garden are suitable for places where there is little else to distract attention: the large seed heads of *Chasmanthium latifolium*, the delicacy of *Melica* species or the delicate variegation of *Carex morrowii* 'Variegata'. Positioning near to seating is always a good idea with plants like this. Grasses that start into growth and flower late are not so good where space is limited. More valuable are compact species that are evergreen or that grow early in the season. The low but elegant *Hakonechloa macra* has become a favourite with many garden designers for this reason; its habit makes it suitable for trailing slightly over walls.

Whatever their size, plants chosen for small spaces do need to be those that do not

spread rapidly, or if they are, they must be contained. Pots from which the bottoms have been removed or tube-like building materials, such as terracotta flue liners, are often a practicable and attractive way of growing a plant while limiting its sideways spread. Less attractive materials can be used below ground.

SHADE

Grasses, as we have seen, are amazingly tolerant of a very wide range of conditions, more so than almost any other groups of garden plants. But reduced light is their Achilles' heel. Their highly efficient photosynthesis mechanism, which is one reason for their global dominance, is rendered largely ineffective out of direct sunlight. Walk from any area of grass, meadow or lawn under trees, and you will notice how rapidly the grass thins out. In full shade it dies out completely.

There are just a few true grasses that are tolerant of light shade; *Milium effusum* flourishes, as do the various graceful species of *Melica*, which we have already met in Groundcover (*see page* 65). But the relatively delicate species of *Melica* need to be grown *en masse* to be effective and to survive the competition of more aggressively spreading shade-tolerant plants, and so they are only really useful as groundcover rather than part of anything more spectacular. The somewhat chunkier *Chasmanthium latifolium* tolerates some shade and makes a good contrast to more graceful species.

Looking beyond the true grasses though, we find a good number of sedges that thrive in the shade of trees and buildings: the dark green leafy *Carex muskingumens*, for example, or the solid clumps of *C. pendula*, or the lower-growing *C. plantaginea*. These are all evergreen and can be combined with other shade-loving plants to provide a rich tapestry of different leaf shapes; one of the joys of gardening in shade is the greater variety of leaf shapes and textures available. The fact that they are evergreen is very useful for maintaining interest through the year, especially since shade plants tend to be spring or early summer flowering, with little happening later on. Variegated ones like *C. morrowii* 'Variegata' are useful for bringing in some light at all times.

The woodrushes, species of *Luzula*, are also evergreen and shade tolerant, doing far better in dry shade than many other plants. They are quite useful to use as a matrix, that is, to form the bulk of a planting, but mixed in with smaller numbers of other, more immediately attractive plants, perhaps hellebores, bulbs, digitalis, the late-flowering white *Aster divaricatus*, or in more moist shade, ferns and hostas.

Bamboos are potentially very useful plants for light shade, but only if the soil never dries out. Shrubs often do not flourish in shade, but bamboos offer a good alternative if height and bulk are needed. Those with running roots, like species of *Sasa*, can be put to good use if there are large areas that need to be filled. Those that do not run, but form tighter clumps, are perfect for those shady situations that need filling upward but not outward, as often happens around buildings, walls and next to paths. The wide variety of foliage, shape and texture among bamboos makes them exceptionally rewarding plants to bring a sense of style to shade.

BELOW FAR LEFT: *Carex pendula* is an unusual plant that is remarkably good for difficult dry shade.

BELOW CENTRE LEFT: *Luzula nivea* forms a carpet of narrow evergreen foliage in shade.

BELOW LEFT: *Luzula sylvatica* is the most robust of the woodrushes for use as groundcover.

BELOW: *Deschampsia cespitosa* 'Goldschleier' is a cultivar of a species that does well in dry light shade and, if densely planted, it makes effective groundcover.

GRASSES IN CONTAINERS

The use of ornamental grasses in containers is a relatively novel approach, but one which has immense potential. Flowering plants in containers tend to be stuffed in cheek by jowl, a situation that often leads to a sense of overcrowding, hence the long-standing use of strongly coloured foliage plants to complement them. Grasses can play a similar complementary role, either through their foliage colour, or the form of the flower/seed head or, indeed, the form of the whole plant.

The fact that many grasses have an arching habit makes them eminently suitable for container culture anyway: the shape often looks just right in a pot, with no other plants needing to be involved, unlike stiffly upright or trailing plants, which always need at least one other shape with them to complement them. Those with fine leaves that can infiltrate and mix together with the stems and flower heads of other pot denizens are the most useful. Those that form squat clumps or have stiff or broad leaves are much less so. Their long period of interest is a great help at the beginning and the end of the season, before and after flowering plants are at their best, and to provide continuity through the waxing and waning of the flowering species.

Fresh young growth or evergreen leaves in spring make a good complement to flowering bulbs and early perennials or bedding plants, such as polyanthus and *Bellis perennis*, or daisies. The yellowy-green young leaves of *Carex elata* 'Aurea' or *Milium effusum* 'Aureum' combine especially well with the intense blues of *Scilla* or *Muscari*, the grape hyacinths. Blues are also effective next to dark bronze colours, such as that of the leaves of the sedge *Uncinia rubra*.

Summer containers can be enlivened with a huge variety of grasses. Annual grasses may be grown from seed or divisions, or young plants of perennial species can be used, although it is vital that the latter are not strongly spreading, otherwise you will end up with a pot of grass and nothing else. Certain annuals are notable for their highly

FAR LEFT: If they are kept well watered, bamboos make very good container plants. This is *Pseudosasa japonica* 'Tsutsumiana'.

CENTRE LEFT: *Hakenochloa macra* 'Aureola' (far left) works well as an accompaniment to gravel and plants in pots.

BELOW LEFT: *Carex morrowii* 'Variegata' is a cultivar whose neat shape lends itself to container cultivation.

LEFT: Container growing is recommended for those who worry about the invasive habits of many bamboos, such as *Sasaella masamuneana* f. *albostriata*.

distinctive large seed heads, such as *Briza maxima*, or conversely for panicles of very fine seed heads, which form clouds among the more clearly defined shapes of flowers; examples include *Briza minor* and *Agrostis nebulosa*.

The pastel colour combinations favoured by many can be given an extra dimension with the striking blue leaves of *Elymus magellanicus*, or the pale fawn, intensely fluffy seed heads of *Pennisetum alopecuroides*. Warmer colour combinations can include any of the bronze or yellow sedges such as *Carex dipsacea*, or, if the container is large enough, the horizontally banded golden variegation of *Miscanthus sinensis* 'Strictus'.

Evergreen grasses are particularly important in winter. *Carex morrowii* 'Evergold' is good not just because of its colour, but because its expansive shape makes up for what the rather squat or ground-hugging winter flowers, such as pansies or heathers, lack.

ORIENTAL STYLE

Bamboos have a particularly strong association with the Far East, although they are far more widely distributed than this. Their role in the gardens of China, Japan and Korea, and in the arts of these countries, accounts for this association, and it is thus rather obvious a point that using bamboo seems to be a vital element in creating oriental-style gardens. However, far too many pastiche gardens have been made that bear little resemblance to the nobility of the originals, and depend too much on the almost knee-jerk reaction so many westerners have: bamboo equals Japan/China. The best oriental gardens are those which contain none of the obvious plants, but local species chosen for the way they echo the spirit of traditional oriental plants. An alternative is to be inspired by the style of oriental gardens, but to develop gardens that do not pretend to be like them but that share certain characteristics, such as simplicity or elegance. Such has been the approach of those few contemporary designers who have made success-ful gardens for modern architectural surroundings.

Grasses can play a vital role in both approaches. Those who have really understood what Japanese gardens are all about, rather than the superficial form they take, will select plants on the basis of a certain, very difficult to define, elegance and economy of form. Grasses, bereft of colourful flowers, are eminently suitable for such gardens. *Miscanthus sinensis* is a native Far Eastern plant, and it often appears in Japanese prints, and yet is far less readily associated with China and Japan than is bamboo, making it ideal for subtle suggestion. Its graceful one-sided flower/seed panicles are invaluable in autumn and winter. *Carex pendula*, with its catkin-like heads pendent on wiry stems, is a good example of the kind of plant that makes a statement based on understatement. The *Melica* grasses are too, and they have the advantage that they grow well in shade.

Courtyards, where few plants are used, are the perfect place to draw attention to subtle details. One clump of grass that may go unnoticed elsewhere could be centre of attention, or play a role in counterpointing something else. In such situations, the interplay between form and texture of plants and the surroundings – fences, walls and surfaces – is all the more important.

OPPOSITE: *Hakonechloa macra* 'Aureola' grows alongside bronze sedges in a Japanese-style garden.

ABOVE LEFT: *Arrhenatherum elatius* subsp. *bulbosum* 'Variegatum' is a grass that is particularly effective in spring.

ABOVE CENTRE: *Milium effusum* 'Aureum' also looks its best in spring.

ABOVE RIGHT: *Carex morrowii* 'Variegata' tolerates light shade.

RIGHT: Trimmed bamboos kept in shape make a traditional-style edging.

ABOVE: *Cyperus* grows against a background of clipped bamboo in mid-winter.

BELOW: The young growth of *Holcus mollis* 'Albovariegatus' spreads among pebbles and gravel.

BELOW RIGHT: Cultivars of *Miscanthus sinensis* are an essential part of modern style. This is 'Flamingo'.

BELOW FAR RIGHT: *Pennisetum alopecuroides* 'Herbstzauber' is one of many highly effective Pennisetum, that tend to do best in continental climates.

CONTEMPORARY STYLE

One of the striking things about grasses is how recent is their entry into the garden. I have come across a reference to using ornamental grasses in an 1880s magazine, but the writer was clearly a voice in the wilderness, and it was not until the 1950s that gardeners in the US and Germany started using the perennial species, with real popularity not coming until much later. They are thus inescapably contemporary plants.

One of the things I love about grasses is the way they fit so well into contemporary environments. They have a simplicity and purity of form that blends well with modern architecture or abstract sculpture, softening the hard outlines of glass and steel buildings and introducing a note of nature into urban places. It is no coincidence that bamboos and certain grasses, notably *Miscanthus sinensis*, were frequently portrayed by Japanese artists and it is Japanese gardens that have inspired much of the best contemporary garden and landscape design. Traditional Japanese art captured the way these plants move so well, and it is their almost constant motion in the slightest breath of wind that makes them so valuable in the vicinity of buildings. The absence of a wide range of colour in traditional Japanese gardens makes us concentrate on the form of plants, and much the same is true of modern-style gardens; a few especially elegant plants are chosen and combined with natural elements like pebbles or weathered wood or manufactured ones such as paving.

It is one of the special qualities of grasses that they are equally effective used *en masse* or as individuals. Those with a strong form, like *Miscanthus* or *Stipa*, are as highly effective in planters in a tiny roof garden as in great masses along a driveway or around a building. The effects created will be different, but both will be equally striking. It was the Brazilian landscape architect Roberto Burle Marx who developed the most truly modernist garden style, using plants in ways designed to emphasize the contrasts they had with each other as strikingly as possible. Oehme and van Sweden in the United States have very much followed in his footsteps, using large quantities of grasses like *Miscanthus*, *Pennisetum* or *Calamagrostis* to contrast with drifts of flowering perennials or shrubs. But they also know when to use individuals or small quantities to equally great effect, for example using three clumps of *Molinia* in a drift of low-growing *Sedum spectabile*, the arching stems making an airy contrast with the colourful but undeniably dumpy sedums. It is this playing off a limited number of different plants against each other that contributes such dynamic creative energy to the best contemporary gardens.

RIGHT: *Calamagrostis* x *acutiflora* 'Karl Foerster' makes an effective upright statement over a long season.

BELOW: A variety of grasses combine effectively with perennials in late summer in the garden of Dutch designer Piet Oudolf.

BOTTOM: *Miscanthus sinensis* 'Malepartus' rise above a carpet of *Carex muskingumensis* in a bracelet of brick and yew, a highly effective and simple modern design by Piet Oudolf.

OPPOSITE: The bromes are all
attractive grasses, somewhat
underrated commercially—this is
Bromus rigidus. They tend to be
short-lived, but are easily
propagated by seed.

RIGHT: The canes of the bamboo
Phyllostachys edulis var.
heterocycla 'Kikko' are very
strangely shaped. It is
hardy only in areas with
a mild winter.

HERE WE LOOK IN DETAIL AT THE BEST OF THE
MORE WIDELY AND EASILY AVAILABLE GRASSES,
BAMBOOS, SEDGES AND WOODRUSHES. THIS
DIRECTORY LISTS OLD FAVOURITES AS WELL AS
TRYING TO GIVE A FLAVOUR OF THE FUTURE —
THIS IS A VERY DYNAMIC AREA IN GARDENING,
AND MORE GOOD VARIETIES APPEAR EVERY YEAR.

DIRECTORY

ALL NON-BAMBOOS ARE DECIDUOUS
UNLESS OTHERWISE INDICATED.
BAMBOOS (B) ARE ALL EVERGREEN.
FIGURES FOR HEIGHT (H) AND
SPREAD (S) INDICATE A PLANT'S
MAXIMUM SIZE WHEN FULLY GROWN.

1

2

ACHNATHERUM BRACHYTRICHA

(SYN. CALAMAGROSTIS BRACHYTRICHUM OR STIPA BRACHYTRICHUM)

Pale brown flower/seed heads with a mauve tinge in late summer and autumn over clumps of fresh green foliage. H 80cm x S 50cm.

CULTIVATION: Most fertile soils in full sun.

USES: Effective with *Monarda* in mid- to late summer or purple and yellow perennials for later on.

SIMILAR VARIETIES: *A. calamagrostis* has more romantically drooping, yellower seed heads.

ALOPECURUS PRATENSIS 'AUREOVARIEGATUS'

Foxtail grass

Orange-yellow and green striped foliage forms mounds. Poker-like flowers are tinted purple in early summer. H 20cm x S 40cm.

CULTIVATION: Full sun or very light shade in fertile soil that does not bake.

USES: Edging or low carpets. Shallow containers. Plant with *Festuca* or *Ophiopogon planiscapus* 'Nigrescens'.

ARUNDO DONAX

Giant reed

Huge grey-green leaves often 75cm long. Large autumn plumes of red-tinted panicles on mature plants if left unpruned, in warmer climates only. H 3–5m x S 1–3m.

CULTIVATION: Any fertile and moist but well-drained soil in full sun. Tolerant of wind and heat once established. Will withstand frost to –10°C.

USES: Windbreak for coastal gardens. Feature plant for combining with other large-leaved plants.

BASHANIA FARGESII (B)

Distinct grey glaucous canes, eventually thick. Medium pointed leaves on short rigid horizontal branches. A very drought-tolerant bamboo with a deeper root structure than most. Establishes quickly even in dry, stony soil.

3

H 3–4m x S 3–5m.

CULTIVATION: Full sun, but will tolerate semi-shade. Spreads quickly with plenty of moisture.

USES: Screening, large grove or windbreak.

BRIZA MEDIA

Perennial quaking grass

Short and clumping with many heart-shaped golden florets held above fine green leaves. H 30cm x S 60cm

CULTIVATION: Form dense colonies through slow spread and self-seeding. Dislikes competition. Easy in fertile soil in sun or light shade. Does best on dry limestone soils.

USES: Good wild garden grass or underplanting for taller grasses, perennials or shrubs. Combine with *Deschampsia*, *Geranium* and *Heuchera*.

BROMUS INERMIS 'SKINNER'S GOLD'

Brome

Very bright yellow-green foliage and tall drooping yellow flowers on pale creamy stalks in mid-summer.
H 90cm x S 1m.
Cultivation: Poor soils will keep the plant short, refined and colourful. Full sun.
Uses: Wild areas, mixed borders or dense grass plantings. Use as a foreground to *Calamagrostis* or *Miscanthus*, so it will brighten the early foliage of these late-flowering plants. Also striking with purple hazel or *Rosa glauca*.

CALAMAGROSTIS X ACUTIFLORA 'KARL FOERSTER'

Reed grass

Dark narrow foliage is topped by stiff, upright bronze-purple flower spikes, which age to buff-grey. Stands winter and winds well.
H 2m x S 90cm.
Cultivation: Moisture-retentive soil in sun.
Uses: Background, screen or focal point. Group with lower-growing perennials, e.g. *Hemerocallis* or *Geranium*, or interplant with other looser-growing grasses.
Similar varieties: *C. x acutiflora* 'Stricta' is almost identical to 'Karl Foerster'. *C. x acutiflora* 'Overdam' is variegated.

CAREX

Sedge

Large genus with 2000 species from a wide range of habitats. Species vary in shape and size from short, dense, tussock-forming plants suitable for large rock gardens or screes to more robust wilderness plants for bog gardens or meadows.

CAREX ATRATA

Stiff, blue-grey evergreen leaves forming dense carpets. Dark purple flowers produce jet-black seed heads that will last throughout the summer.
H 45cm x S 60cm.

Cultivation: Full sun or open aspect in light shade, average to moist soil.
Uses: Gravel-mulched areas, containers or low carpeting. The short leaves look effective at a pond edge with irises.
Similar varieties: *C. caryophyllea* 'The Beatles' is similar in habit but forms a tighter clump.

CAREX COMANS

Arching pale brown delicate hair-like foliage forms dense evergreen tufts.
H 30cm x S 60cm.
Cultivation: Full sun in average soil.
Uses: Very versatile. Use in containers, mixed planting or *en masse* with other grasses. Good with bronzes, blues and purples.
Similar varieties: The bronze form of *C. comans* is shorter, with dusky chocolate-brown foliage. *C.* 'Frosted Curls' is taller with unique blond colouring. *C. flagellifera* has deep chestnut-brown hair-like foliage.

[1] *Achnatherum brachytricha* is a first-rate medium-sized grass.

[2] *Arundo donax* is a hardy giant reed from the tropics.

[3] *Bashania fargesii* has characteristic leaf pleating.

[4] *Briza media* is a species of thin limestone grassland.

[5] *Calamagrostis x acutiflora* 'Karl Foerster' has a long season of interest.

[6] The rich brown foliage of the bronze form of *Carex comans* is much appreciated in winter.

CAREX ELATA 'AUREA'
Tufted sedge

Rich golden-edged, long narrow leaves for early spring and summer colour on tight, slowly spreading clumps. Dark brown flowers in early summer.
H 70cm x S 40cm.
CULTIVATION: Sun or light shade, moist soil or pond margins.
USES: Best admired as a solitary specimen.

CAREX HACHIJOENSIS

Rich glossy evergreen leaves, strong and slightly arching. Pale flowers.
H 40cm x S 40cm.
CULTIVATION: Most soils, sun or shade.
USES: This species and similar variegated forms (below) are good low cover in between larger, clump-forming grasses or other low perennial planting.

CAREX MORROWII 'VARIEGATA'

Pale, subtle variegation creates an all-over milky-green colour. Rigid evergreen leaves, slightly arching.
H 35cm x S 50cm.
CULTIVATION: Full sun or shade, moist or dry soil.
USES: Will cover ground under dark evergreens with ample watering to establish young plants. Useful basal planting for bamboos or as formal path edge planting.

CAREX MUSKINGUMENSIS
Palm sedge

Exotic-looking foliage with tall stems and thin leaves arching horizontally with a palm-like effect. Deciduous.
H 80cm x S 50cm.
CULTIVATION: Moist shady areas or in the bog garden, although it will tolerate average soil conditions.
USES: Focal point or groundcover in wild or marginal grass plantings. Bold colours contrast well.

CAREX PENDULA
Weeping sedge

One of the largest sedges, with broad-pleated, semi-evergreen leaves, long and arching. Red-brown catkin-like flowers in spring hang from tall arching stems.
H 90cm x S 90cm.
CULTIVATION: Moist and rich soil in dappled shade, but likes full sun if kept moist. Can self-seed too generously.
USES: Woodland path edging or waterside wild gardens; interplant large drifts with foxgloves or columbines.

CAREX PLANTAGINEA

Tightly clumping evergreen with broad, pleated leaves up to 2.5cm wide, with striking spikes of rusty red and black flowers.
H 30cm x S 40cm.
CULTIVATION: Best suited to shady woodland, if not too dry. Also rewarding in pots, given ample food and water.
USES: Superb edging to woodland paths or shady pools, alongside *Epimedium*, *Pulmonaria*, *Erythronium* and ferns.
SIMILAR VARIETIES: Though deciduous, *C. siderosticha* 'Variegata' is similar to *C. plantaginea*, with bold white-striped and margined leaves.

CAREX RIPARIA 'VARIEGATA'
Greater pond sedge

Early spring growth is almost completely white, toning to a milky green as the season advances. The early almost jet-black flowers are a sharp contrast. Striking, desirable and easy, but very invasive.
H 50cm x S 1m.
CULTIVATION: Sun or light shade is necessary for the brilliant colour. Tolerant of all except the driest soils and well suited to bog conditions.
USES: As a bold and spreading feature on large pond margins where it will bind the soil. Usually too vigorous to combine with other plants, unless they are equally robust, e.g. *Gunnera* species or *Ligularia*.

CAREX TESTACEA

Tight evergreen clumps of olive-green hair-like foliage. The colour turns a darker orange-red in full sun in winter.
H 40cm x S 60cm.
CULTIVATION: Resents hard pruning when mature. Full sun in moist, free-draining soil.
USES: Tumbles over raised beds or rocks. Compact source of colour in winter, or with yellow or blue bulbs in spring.
SIMILAR VARIETIES: *C. dipsacea* is very similar but is more tolerant of wetter conditions.

CHASMANTHIUM LATIFOLIUM
Spangle grass, sea oats

Slowly spreading clumps of broad deciduous leaves. Flat spikes of green flowers turn copper and then grey as the foliage simultaneously changes to pink and straw yellow.
H 90cm x S 60cm.
CULTIVATION: Good soil in light shade is ideal. Will grow in full sun but requires more moisture.
USES: Fine winter garden plant – looks superb in frost.

CHIMONOBAMBUSA MARMOREA (B)

Marble bamboo

Loose clumps of pale green canes turn plum-purple, with small twisted leaves in dense bunches at the ends. New shoots are strikingly marbled.
H 1m 80cm x S 3m.

CULTIVATION: Naturally grove forming, but is relatively easy to control because of shallow rooting. Needs good soil, well mulched, in sun or part shade.

USES: A versatile plant for waterside or wild places. Fine and easily manageable in containers.

SIMILAR VARIETIES: *C. tumidissinoda* is elegant but invasive, ideal for pot culture, growing to 3m in a bed, 1m in pots.

CHIONOCHLOA RUBRA

Tussock grass

Narrow ochre-red, evergreen leaves forming dense arching clumps with good red and pink winter tints.
H 75cm x S 30cm.

CULTIVATION: Slow to establish. Likes sun in good, well-drained soil.

USES: The essential winter garden plant. Use with dwarf pines and prostrate blue junipers. Some beach pebbles and driftwood will add background grey tones to the orange, blues and greens.

CHONDROSUM GRACILE

(SYN. BOUTEOUA GRACILE)

Mosquito grass

Unusual flower heads grow at right angles to the vertical stems, silvery at first and then turning purple.
H 40cm x S 40cm.

CULTIVATION: Well-drained soil in an open aspect.

USES: Best used as underplanting around established shrubs which will take up any moisture quickly, providing the ideal soil conditions for this grass.

CHUSQUEA CULEOU (B)

A bold and desirable clump-forming species with thick, yellow-green solid canes, often purple-black when young. Dense, rigid clusters of short, dark evergreen leaves form bottle-brush formations on the upper half of the canes.
H 6m x S 3m.

CULTIVATION: Good drainage and an open aspect in sun.

USES: One of the boldest features for a medium to large garden and deserves a prominent placing. Underplanting will spoil the effect of the new emerging canes.

5

6

4

[1] Elegant *Carex morrowii* 'Variegata' is a widely available sedge.

[2] A unique pattern of growth makes *Carex muskingumensis* a valuable and distinctive ornamental plant.

[3] *Carex pendula* is a tough survivor for difficult areas, especially shade.

[4] *Carex riparia* 'Variegata' is normally a vigorous species, but the variegation of this cultivar reduces its growth rate.

[5] *Chimonobambusa tumidissinoda* is traditionally used for making walking sticks.

[6] *Chusquea culeou* is probably the best of the tight clump-forming bamboos.

CORTADERIA SELLOANA

Pampas grass

A variable species. Coarse evergreen, arching foliage with huge silky white plumes standing well above the foliage during autumn.
H 3m x S 1m.

CULTIVATION: All forms require a sunny aspect in well-drained soil, not too poor. Hard pruning in spring helps to keep the plant tidy. Very tolerant of salt and exposure to cold winds.

USES: Large groups can be very effective. Helps to brighten up the foreground of large, formal evergreen hedges and the monotony of huge areas of lawn. Drifts of *Bergenia* are a good complement or use it as spot planting with *Yucca*, *Phormium*, purple *Euphorbia* (spurges) and *Kniphofia*.

CULTIVARS: *Cortaderia selloana* 'Aureolineata' (syn. *C. s* 'Gold Band') has excellent gold-margined foliage on upright clumps. *C. s.* 'Sunningdale Silver' has enormous silvery-white plumes held well above the foliage.

CYPERUS ERAGROSTIS

Umbrella sedge

Strong clumps of rich green foliage, with deeply veined leaves and large umbels of yellow-green flowers in summer and autumn.
ZH 60cm x S 60cm.

CULTIVATION: Withstands sun or shade, boggy or ordinary soil. Annual tidying and thinning of self-sown seedlings may be necessary.

USES: Pond or lake margins in large groups with other marginal plants. Allow it to seed itself in the larger gravel garden or plant in containers near small formal pools or on the patio.

DESCHAMPSIA CESPITOSA

Hairgrass

The densely tufted evergreen foliage is neat and fresh and the early-maturing golden or bronze flowers last for the greater part of the year.
H 1m x S 40cm.

CULTIVATION: Light shade with fertile, moist soil is ideal. Divide occasionally and shear annually in winter.

USES: Plant in large drifts or use for spot planting. Extremely versatile, looking good almost anywhere. Combine with hostas, *Polygonatum* (Solomon's seal) and broader-leaved grasses.

CULTIVARS: *Deschampsia cespitosa* 'Bronzeschleier' has dark, rusty-brown arching flowers and is taller than most cultivars. *D. c.* 'Goldtau' is shorter, with stiff spikes of pale golden flowers lasting for ages and compact dark green foliage. *D.c.* 'Goldshleier' is quite tall, with golden flower heads.

DESCHAMPSIA FLEXUOSA

Wavy hairgrass

Very fine-leaved and tufted species thriving best in cool climates where the evergreen, shiny, needle-like foliage stays lush. The flowers erupt from the foliage up to 35cm and turn rich purple-brown.
H 35cm x S 40cm.

CULTIVATION: Easy and adaptable in all except the most arid conditions, and good on acid soils. Can self-seed.

USES: Good companion to heathers and other low-growing plants tolerant of acid soils.

CULTIVARS: *D .f.* 'Tatra Gold' is a shorter golden-green form, very bright in spring.

ELYMUS HISPIDUS

Wild rye, lyme grass

Erect leaves of a stunning silver-blue on young growth, arching later in the season. Wheat-like flowers. Clump-forming and not invasive, like many others in this genus.
H 1m x S 40cm.

CULTIVATION: A dry stony site with full sun will really bring out the vivid colour.

USES: Dry gravel gardens or sandy areas. Good against a dark background of timber palisades or plants such as purple *Cotinus*, purple-leaved vines or dark-leaved ivies.

SIMILAR VARIETIES: *E. magellanicus* is also a startling blue but it is short lived, although it self-seeds fairly reliably. Other species (and the closely related *Leymus*) are often terribly invasive.

ERIOPHORUM ANGUSTIFOLIUM

Common cotton grass

Dark, emerald foliage often tinted dark red. Small flower spikes produce striking bunches of cotton-like heads up to 6cm long. Vigorous spreading habit.
H 40cm x S 60cm.
CULTIVATION: Only produces the cotton heads reliably when used in boggy, acidic soils. Sun or light shade.
USES: Wild pond margins and bog gardens. *Caltha* and *Lysichiton* will add contrast.
SIMILAR VARIETIES: *Eriophorum latifolium* has similar flowers but is more clumping and is tolerant of calcareous soils.

FARGESIA (B)

A genus of tight clump-forming bamboos. The canes are usually strong and upright, with a canopy of of fresh, small leaves, often glaucous.

[1] *Deschampsia cespitosa* 'Goldschleier' is an attractive cultivar for light dry shade and poor soil.

[2] *Deschampsia flexuosa* 'Tatra Gold' really thrives on poor acid soils.

[3] *Elymus magellanicus* is a lovely blue-grey. Unlike other *Elymus* it does not run.

[4] *Eriophorum angustifolium* is best grown in a bog garden on acid soils.

[5] *Fargesia nitida* 'Nymphenburg' has a fine arching habit, ideal for a tunnel effect.

[6] Many fescues, like *Festuca glauca*, have fine blue-grey foliage and a tight clump-forming habit.

FARGESIA MURIELIAE

Umbrella bamboo

The most common bamboo in cultivation. Thin green canes turn orange-yellow with age and hold aloft a mass of pale evergreen leaves.
H 4m x S 1m.
CULTIVATION: Very easy to grow in sites that never dry out.
USES: As a central specimen, screen or container plant. Underplant with low evergreen cover such as *Waldsteinia* or *Vinca* to keep the canes and wonderful habit in view.
SIMILAR VARIETIES: *Fargesia nitida* is tightly clump-forming with dark purple young canes, branching in the second year with many thin, pointed, glaucous leaves (H 3.5m x S 1m).

FESTUCA

Fescue

Mostly blue or glaucous green in colour and tightly clump-forming with thread-like evergreen leaves.

FESTUCA AMETHYSTINA

Sheep's fescue, tufted fescue

Densely tufted blue-green thin foliage. Very noticeable fawn flowers in spring.
H 35cm x S 25cm.
CULTIVATION: Full sun in free-draining soil. Annual shearing after flowering keeps them tidy. Older plants can be divided at this time if they begin to lose vigour.
USES: Edging for borders, group planting or containers, with *Bergenia* or tidy and low rock garden plants.
SIMILAR VARIETIES: *F. glauca* 'Harz' has turquoise foliage, tinted pink. *F. curvula* subsp. *crassifolia* has a more open habit with steel-blue summer growth (H 50cm x S 40cm.)

FESTUCA GLAUCA

Blue fescue, grey fescue

Pale blue erect thread-like leaves and dense clusters of blue-green flowers turning straw yellow.
H 40cm x S 30cm.
CULTIVATION: Full sun in open aspect, not crowded.
USES: For bed edging with *Diascia*, *Helianthemum*, thymes or other creepers. Looks striking when massed in old red clay pots among pebbles and taller container planting.
SIMILAR VARIETIES: There are many to choose from this varied species and the similar *F. ovina* and *F. valesiaca*. *F. v.* 'Silbersee' is slow-growing, very bright blue, with short, grey-blue flowers with a pincushion habit.
CULTIVARS: *F. glauca* 'Azurit' has a small habit and brighter blue growth, but is shy to flower.

5

6

GLYCERIA MAXIMA VAR. VARIEGATA

Reed grass, sweet grass

Vertical leaves, heavily striped cream and white with pink-flushed new growth. A very colourful and worthwhile plant all year.
H 8m x S indefinite.
CULTIVATION: Prefers moist, boggy conditions or even shallow water, but will tolerate good garden soil.
USES: Deserves to be planted in very large groups by the waterside but can look equally at home in large containers plunged in shallow ponds.

HAKONECHLOA MACRA

Hakone grass

Slow growing with long, narrow, bamboo-like leaves tapering to a point on long stalks arching from tight clumps, maturing to a delicate pink and red in late summer. Deciduous.
H 40cm x S 60cm.
CULTIVATION: Requires cool, moist and rich root conditions in well-drained soil, ideally in light shade. Hot sun and dry weather may burn the leaves.
USES: Very versatile and can be used almost anywhere with a multitude of plants. Good with late-flowering perennials and white-variegated hostas.
CULTIVARS: *H. m.* 'Aureola' has slow-growing clumps of beautiful yellow and pale green striped leaves with an arching habit, red autumn tints and darker flowers. The leaves of *H. m.* 'Mediovariegata' are finely striped and margined with creamy-white, producing a silvery effect.

HELICTOTRICHON SEMPERVIRENS

Blue oat grass

Arching tufts of narrow, blue-grey leaves. Flowers in mid-summer, quickly turning rich golden-brown.
H 1m x S 60cm.
CULTIVATION: Well-drained, rich soil in sun, not crowded by other plants. Careful pruning of the older evergreen leaves when new shoots appear is preferable to general shearing. Tolerant of very alkaline soils.
USES: A fine accent plant or for group planting if well spaced. Adds unusual form and colour to low perennial borders. Particularly good with silver *Artemisia*.

x HIBANOBAMUSA TRANQUILLANS (B)

Large-veined evergreen leaves taper to a point and can measure 20cm long by 7cm wide. The foliage effect is deep, glossy green, staying fresh through the winter.
H 2.5m x S 1.5m .
CULTIVATION: Tolerant of sun or shade in moist but free-draining soil.
USES: Very useful, suited to screening or specimen use.

HYSTRIX PATULA

Bottlebrush grass

Although normally grown for the spiky, pale silver flowers, which last well into winter, the foliage is also attractive, often tinted red in early spring and again in late summer after flowering.
H 90cm x S 40cm.
CULTIVATION: Prefers moist, well-drained soil in part shade. Deciduous.
USES: Naturalize in woodland gardens or plant around large-leafed bamboos. Looks good with low plants, e.g. *Persicaria affinis* 'Superba' or *Geranium sanguineum*.

[1] *Glyceria maxima* var. *variegata* is an aggressive spreader unless contained.

[2] *Hakonechloa macra* is largely grown for its neat foliage and habit.

[3] *Helictotrichon sempervirens* is a rewarding species that is fairly tolerant of most soils.

[4] *Juncus effusus* is a common species rarely grown in gardens, but with potential for its straight foliage.

IMPERATA CYLINDRICA 'RUBRA'
Japanese blood grass

Thin, almost translucent vertical growth with narrow evergreen leaves. Bright green spring growth gradually changes on the upper half of the foliage to a deep blood red, which stays through winter.
H 40cm x S 20cm.
Cultivation: Difficult to establish unless soil conditions are perfect. Needs rich moisture-retentive soil in full sun where it will spread slowly.
Uses: On raised beds, background light will enhance the colour and translucence of the foliage. Useful in pots to mix with other plants, especially variegated ones.

INDOCALAMUS LATIFOLIUS (B)

Moderate spreader with thin but strong canes and large evergreen glossy leaves on single branches. Extremely ornamental and tolerant of wind once established.
H 2m x S 1m.
Cultivation: Light shade in moist humus-rich soil. Older growth may be thinned to keep open and tidy.
Uses: Fine when established against a shaded wall or under tall canopied trees. Low planting with *Corydalis* or *Pulmonaria* can protect the soil from drying out around the base. Useful for creating the exotic look.
Similar varieties: *I. solidus* is shorter, but otherwise similar in habit, with tougher and darker green foliage. *I. tessellatus* is very tropical looking with massive plate-sized leaves when mature.

JUNCUS EFFUSUS 'SPIRALIS'
Corkscrew rush

A neat curiosity with semi-evergreen coiled and twisted, cylindrical green foliage. The shoots tangle and mat together to form a tight clump.
H 40cm x S 40cm.
Cultivation: Shallow water or boggy soil. Old plants become congested but are easily split and grow freshly.
Uses: An unusual feature in containers with constant moisture. Plant with *Iris sibirica*, *Acorus* or *Houttuynia*.
Similar varieties: The parent species has straight foliage.

KOELERIA GLAUCA
Blue hairgrass

Similar in habit to blue *Festuca* but stronger in form and leaf size. Hedgehog-like tussocks of pale turquoise evergreen leaves arching from a central crown. The pale blue-grey flowers rise just above the foliage in June.
H 30cm x S 20cm.
Cultivation: Tolerant of dry, even chalky, sites in full sun or exposure. Late summer tidying encourages another flush of leaves. Deciduous. Thrives on regular division.
Uses: For the dry gravel or rock garden in bold groups. Foreground planting or edging to narrow borders with *Acaena* and dwarf *Campanula*.

LAGURUS OVATUS
Hare's tail

A bold and useful annual grass with soft, bushy flower heads of a delicate whitish green.
H 60cm x S 30cm.
Cultivation: Light sandy soil in full sun. Tolerant of drought once established. Seed should be collected and sown *in situ* in succession in spring for summer flowers.
Uses: Mostly grown for drying and floral arrangements but useful in a sunny border.

LUZULA NIVEA
Snowy woodrush

Small-growing and highly ornamental evergreen with downy grey-green foliage. Fluffy white flowers in spring toning to a pale rusty cream.
H 45cm x S 30cm.
Cultivation: Easy and adaptable to a wide range of soils and conditions. Sun or shade and tolerant of some drought when established, even of the difficult root-filled situations around trees. Hard pruning immediately after flowering will provide neat low carpets of the attractive silvery foliage.
Uses: Invaluable as woodland groundcover or as path edging, or as groundcover where almost nothing else will grow. Combine with other low shade-loving plants such as Euphorbia amygdaloides var. 'Robbiae', or varieties of Vinca and Hedera.
Similar varieties: Luzula lactea is evergreen, with darker foliage and yellow-white flowers later than L. nivea.
L. luzuloides 'Schneehaschen' is more vigorous, but otherwise identical to L. nivea. L. sylvatica (the greater woodrush) is a versatile evergreen, with dense clumps of long narrow pea-green leaves and plentiful golden-brown spring flowers rising through the foliage (H 50cm x S 1m). L. s. 'Aurea' (syn. L. s. 'Hohe Tatra') has pale lime-green summer leaves with a burst of deep lemon-yellow winter colour. L. s. 'Marginata' has finely margined white and green leaves. All are tolerant of dry shade.

MELICA ALTISSIMA 'ATROPURPUREA'
Siberian melic

Soft green arching leaves emerging from tidy clumps provide masses of one-sided purple spikes with a papery appearance. Deciduous but reliably perennial.
H 90cm x S 50cm.
Cultivation: Moist, rich soil in sun or light shade will keep the plant fresh and in flower for ages. Also tolerant of drier conditions.
Uses: Seeds around, and is pleasing alongside a wide variety of perennials, particularly with hardy geraniums, which flower at the same time.

Similar varieties: M. ciliata has a profusion of fluffy, off-white panicles that wave in the slightest breeze.

MILIUM EFFUSUM 'AUREUM'
Bowles' golden grass

Golden-yellow papery leaves hold their colour even in shade. The nodding flowers are delicate pale yellow,
H 30cm x S 60cm.
Cultivation: Tolerant of sun or shade, including dry shade, though more moisture is required when it is grown in hot areas. Slowly spreading clumps will usually multiply by self-seeding.
Uses: Brightens up the dullest corner with an almost fluorescent display. Works particularly well with spring perennials, especially those with blue or purple flowers, which form a pleasing contrast with the yellow foliage.

MISCANTHUS
Silver grass, eulalia

Tall graceful foliage and late summer flowers/seed heads which last well into winter providing almost nine months of striking elegance. There are a great many Miscanthus sinensis cultivars, many of which appear similar as young plants but mature with subtle differences of flower colour, foliage, shape and habit.

MISCANTHUS SACCHARIFLORUS
Silver banner grass, Amur silver grass

Tall, with a sub-tropical appearance. Broad clumps of bamboo-like canes with long arching strappy leaves. Small silver flowers.
H 2.5m x S 1.5m.
Cultivation: Moist fertile soil in full sun. Withstands strong winds even in the winter, when it pales to a rich straw colour.
Uses: Screening or for specimen use as a feature plant or as background planting.
Similar varieties: M. floridulus is slightly more reliably evergreen than M. sacchariflorus, and it has a better display of late colouring.

[1] *Luzula nivea* has fine white hairs on the outermost edges of its leaves which contribute to its interesting and unusual appearance.

[2] *Milium effusum* 'Aureum' is a useful plant to have in the garden because it is one of the minority of grasses whose best season of interest is the early summer.

[3] *Miscanthus sinensis* 'Malepartus' is one of the best of the larger *Miscanthus* cultivars.

[4] *Miscanthus sinensis* 'Morning Light' has cream edging to its leaves.

[5] The delicate flowers of *Miscanthus x oligonensis* 'Zwergelefant' emerge on the stem.

MISCANTHUS SINENSIS
Japanese silver grass, eulalia

Tightly clumping with rigid, vertical stems of long narrow foliage. Autumn tints vary from pale, creamy-yellow through a pink tan to deep orange or purple-red. Flowers on some cultivars appear as early as July and a few as late as October. The whole plant dies off by midwinter. H 1–3m x S 1–1.5m.

Cultivation: Best in rich, moisture-retentive soil but also adaptable to drier sites, which give a shorter habit and earlier flowering. Full sun provides the best flower and foliage colour. Narrow-leaved forms seem more drought tolerant. Hard prune in spring before new growth and occasionally divide (every 5–7 years).

Uses: As screens, focal points or in mixed border planting or as pond edging (but not in boggy soil). Look best accompanied by large late-flowering perennials such as *Aster* and *Helenium*.

Cultivars: *M. s.* 'Kleine Fontäne' has bold red arching flowers from mid- to late summer, turning silver and fluffy, with strong vertical stems and red-tinted foliage late in season (H 2m x S 50cm). *M. s.* 'China' is similar to *M. s.* 'Kleine Fontäne but slightly later. *M. s.* 'Flamingo' has deep claret-red plumes turning pink to silver, narrow foliage and an arching habit. It is strong in the winter (H 1m x S 50cm). *M. s.* 'Gracillimus' is an old cultivar with very fine-textured foliage with silvery midribs. It is pale in growth until autumn, when it will colour with yellow and orange. The flowers are very late and only appear after a long growing season (H 1m x S 20cm). *M. s.* 'Nippon' is similar to *M. s.* 'Gracillimus' with copper autumn tones. *M. s.* 'Graziella' has large silver-white plumes that grow high above the foliage, with good autumn colour in colder climates. It is quick to establish (H 1.7m). *M. s.* 'Undine' is similar, and also easy to establish, but bigger

at 2m. *M. s.* 'Kaskade' has deep purple-brown flowers turning silvery-pink with orange-red autumn leaf colour and an elegant arching habit (H 1.8m). *M. s.* 'Kleine Silberspinne' is a compact plant with very narrow silvery leaves. Dark red-brown plumes like narrow fans appear in mid-summer. It is very stout and lasts longer than most grasses – through winter until pruning. Ideal for the smaller garden (H 1m). *M. s.* 'Silberspinne' is only a little taller than *M. s.* 'Kleine Silberspinne' with a slightly more open habit. *M. s.* 'Malepartus' has large deep red flowers that are slightly arching, strong stems and broad leaves that also turn a rich purple-red (H 2.5m). *M. s.* 'Rotsilber' is similar. *M. s.* 'Morning Light' is slender and similar to *M. s.* 'Gracillimus'. It is shy to flower, with pale leaves delicately margined white for a shimmering effect (H 1m). *M. s.* 'Silberfeder' is very tall with arching pink plumes, quickly turning to silver. The leaves have a broad silvery-white central vein and good yellow autumn colour. It has a strong habit, lasting well into the spring (H 3m or more). *M. s.* 'Strictus' has a tight vertical habit with green leaves horizontally banded yellow. It flowers late but the foliage is tough and almost semi-evergreen, giving late colour (H 2m). *M. s.* 'Variegatus'has broad creamy-white margined leaves and shy red flowers (H 2m). *M. s.* 'Zebrinus' is identical in colouring but more open in habit, with foliage arching at the top (H 3m). *M. s.* 'Pünktchen' is a new dwarfer form with the same yellow banding and more reliable, deep red flowers (H 1.2m). *M. s.* 'Yakushima Dwarf' is a diminutive form, as the name suggests, growing to only 30cm with sporadic dark brown flowers just above the foliage. It forms curious hummocks, with leaves curling at the tips.

Similar varieties: *M. x oligonensis* 'Zwergelefant' has wide leaves and grows to 2m. The name means dwarf elephant, referring to the shape of the young flowers.

MOLINIA CAERULEA
Moor grass

Tufts of narrow foliage and flowers form on straight stems from late summer onwards. All forms are deciduous, and sub-species *arundinacea* types lose their seed heads in early winter.
H 1–2m x S 30–60cm.

CULTIVATION: Moist fertile soil in full sun provides the best results. Very alkaline soils are not tolerated. Clear untidy growth in early spring and divide when clumps start to grow thinly from the crown.

USES: For single specimen accent planting or grouping with other grasses and perennials. The usual bright yellow or orange autumn colouring associates well with other autumn foliage.

CULTIVARS: *M. c.* subsp. *arundinacea* 'Bergfreund' has green strappy leaves, almost vertical in habit, with tall dark purple flowers from late July. Autumn colour is pale yellow (H 1.5m x S 60cm). *M. c.* subsp. *arundinacea* 'Transparent' has strong foliage, and delicate airy flowers on large panicles do give an almost transparent effect, earning it its name. Late summer and autumn foliage is bright yellow, with the stems standing into winter (H 2m x S 60cm). *M. c.* subsp. *caerulea* 'Windspiel' has large panicles of golden flowers held high above glossy green, strap-like leaves. This is another good autumn gold (H 1.8 m x S 50cm). *M. c.* subsp. *caerulea* 'Edith Dudszus' is a shorter form with neat, spiky leaves and dark red stems producing late matt-purple flowers. It has pale creamy-yellow colour in autumn (H 1m x S 30cm). *M. c.* subsp. *caerulea* 'Heidebraut' has broad fountains of narrow foliage and short dark stems of pale flowers. A deep orange-yellow, it turns dark russet-red with the first frosts (H 1m x S 40cm). *M. c.* subsp. *caerulea* 'Moorhexe' is much smaller in stature, forming a tight clump of grey-green pointed leaves. Dark flowers are often produced as early as July (H 80cm x S 30cm). *M. c.* subsp. *caerulea* 'Variegata' is a delightful variegated form with cream and green striped leaves. Very dark flowers appear in July on thin, shiny yellow stems.

MUHLENBERGIA JAPONICA 'CREAM DELIGHT'
Muhly grass

Colourful mat of creamy foliage. Thin white-striped leaves and stems turn buff-yellow in autumn just after the pale silvery flowers appear.
H 20cm x S 1m.

CULTIVATION: Winter tidying and hard spring pruning with division every few years are necessary to keep the plant young and fresh. Sun and average soil.

USES: As a mat around taller grasses such as *Molinia* or *Miscanthus*, or on low walls or rockeries.

PANICUM CLANDESTINUM
Deer-tongue grass

Distinct bright, almost bamboo-like foliage. Soft green leaves, broad and tapering sharply to a point from the reddish stems. Fine russet autumn hues. Compact.
H 90cm x S 75cm.

CULTIVATION: Moist but well-drained soil in light shade.

USES: As woodland path edging or groundcover by pools.

PANICUM VIRGATUM
Switch grass

Clump-forming and upright with long narrow foliage and sprays of tiny silvery or red flowers in loose panicles in late summer.
H 90cm–1m x S 20–45cm.

CULTIVATION: Moisture-retentive soil in sun is ideal but all adapt to poorer conditions once established. Good in wind and salt spray.

USES: Adds character and height to perennial borders and mixes well with other late-season grasses such as *Stipa* or *Miscanthus* and late perennials like *Sedum spectabile* and *Aster*, or low shrubs like *Cotoneaster horizontalis*.

CULTIVARS: *Panicum virgatum* 'Hänse Herms' has deep purple flowers and plum-tinted foliage (H 90cm x S 40cm). *P. v.* 'Rehbraun' is similar but not so good.

P. v. 'Heavy Metal' has metallic-blue vertical leaves that turn pale yellow in autumn and late yellow-brown flower panicles (H 1m x S 20cm). *P. v.* 'Rotstrahlbusch' has deep claret-red autumn colour and dark greeny-red flowers (H 1m x S 45cm).

PENNISETUM ALOPECUROIDES
Fountain grass

Showy deciduous grass forming tight clumps of stiff pointed foliage with many large, pink-tinted, foxtail-like fluffy flowers/seed heads from mid-summer. Autumn foliage tints vary from rich creamy-yellow to pink, depending on the site.
H 1m x S 60cm.

CULTIVATION: Tolerant of most soils, but dislikes winter wet. Full sun or very light shade.

USES: Good autumn and winter effect, the late colours going well with the rich autumn yellows and reds of many shrubs, as well as the yellows and purple-violets of late-flowering perennials. Can be used either as a focal point or in groups.

CULTIVARS: *P. a.* 'Hameln' is dwarf with short rigid flowers. H 50cm x S 30cm. *P. a.* 'Woodside' is compact with a reliable display of flowers. It is tolerant of more shade than the species and other cultivars (H 75cm x S 45cm.)

SIMILAR VARIETIES: *P. orientale* (oriental fountain grass) has pink flowers fading to off-white (H 60cm x S 50cm).

PHALARIS ARUNDINACEA
Ribbon grass, gardeners' garters

Tall grass with bamboo-like foliage, bright glaucous green, paling to warm buff-yellow. Flowers are tall, pink-tinged panicles. Strongly spreading.
H 1m x S 80cm.

CULTIVATION: Very moist soils in sun or light shade; wind and exposure tolerant.

USES: A bold pond-edger tolerating almost bog-like conditions. Suitable only for the larger garden unless regularly thinned. Can be used with *Gunnera* and *Filipendula* to create a controlled wilderness.

SIMILAR VARIETIES: *P. a.* var. *picta* 'Feesey' is the form most suitable for a smaller garden, with an almost completely pure white effect.

[1] *Molinia caerulea* is inconspicuous until it flowers.

[2] *Panicum virgatum* 'Rehbraun' has reddish autumn tints.

[3] *Pennisetum alopecuroides* is good for late summer and autumn interest.

[4] *Pennisetum orientale* has violet-pink flowers that turn to straw-coloured seed heads.

[5] *Phalaris arundinacea* var. *picta* 'Feesey' is a moisture-loving invasive plant with exotic variegation.

PHYLLOSTACHYS (B)

An important and remarkable genus with tall often thick canes with a groove (sulcus) on the sides. New canes (culms) develop taller and thicker as the rhizome below ground matures. The genus has many species, variable in habit. Many are invasive in their natural habitat but are more refined and compact in cooler temperate regions.

PHYLLOSTACHYS AUREA
Fishpole bamboo

Tall, almost vertical habit, foliage held high. Compact unless conditions are wet and warm.
H 5m x S 1.5m.
Cultivation: Rich moist soil. Occasional thinning of older canes will result in stronger growth.
Uses: Ideal specimen plant or screen. Suitable for small gardens due to its vertical habit.

PHYLLOSTACHYS AUREOSULCATA
Crookstem bamboo, yellow grove bamboo

One of the hardiest. Vertical green canes with yellow grooves, often zig-zagging at the base. Small deep green foliage is always fresh and glossy. A moderate runner.
H 5m x S 2.5m.
Cultivation: Occasional thinning necessary to encourage the display of the young canes.
Uses: As edge or pathside planting to appreciate the unusual canes, while large mature groves can be thinned and paths cut through. Heavy stepping stones will divert young shoots and create a narrow bamboo tunnel. The canes of this species and the its golden cultivars should not be congested with intrusive planting or the vertical effect will be lost. Also makes a useful screen or hedge, even in exposed locations.

PHYLLOSTACHYS BAMBUSOIDES
Japanese timber bamboo

Large clumps of very strong thick canes of a rich shiny green. Medium-sized, pointed leaves. Tight in habit until mature, when it forms an open grove of vertical canes.
H 6m x S 2.5m.
Cultivation: Very adaptable in acid or alkaline moisture-retentive soils. In cool regions it is best planted in sun to ripen the late emerging shoots. Older growth needs removing regularly. Can be rampant in warmer areas.
Uses: Ideal for screening or for a bold central feature. In larger gardens where large island beds can be created, *Mahonia* is a good associate.

PHYLLOSTACHYS BISSETII

Rich glossy purple-green new canes and dense foliage quickly form a colony. Older canes turn pale green.
H 5.5m x S 3m.
Cultivation: Any moisture-retentive soil.
Uses: As a screen, hedge or background. Will bind loose banks or the edges of natural ponds. Strands of willows, e.g. *Salix alba* 'Britzensis', with bright winter stems, positively shine against the dark foliage.

PHYLLOSTACHYS NIGRA
Black bamboo

Shiny, jet black canes form tall tidy clumps. The small pale green leaves enhance the dark canes. Young canes, green at first, turn black over a two- or three-year period.
H 5m x S 1.5 m.

Cultivation: Full sun ripens the canes best, but the plants must not dry out. Pruning the lower branches will also allow light to the canes and help ripening.
Uses: Very adaptable and can be used successfully in large containers on patios or balconies. The ideal focus for a small or medium garden, the black colouring is well suited for association with many plants, such as the foliage of *Hedera helix* 'Silver King'. Blue flowers or dark purple foliage are also very effective companions.

PHYLLOSTACHYS VIVAX
Smooth-sheathed bamboo

Tall and stately with very thick pale green canes and a high foliage canopy. Very compact at the base and broad at the top, forming a distinct V-shape. The new culms are striking with dark spotting.
H 6m x S 1.5m.
Cultivation: Young plants will take time to mature and few canes are initially produced until the underground rhizomes develop, the initial growth being thin and juvenile (this is common in many of the taller cane bamboos). Large canes will eventually, after a number of years, supersede the early growth, which can then be removed. Sun or shade.
Uses: A stunning specimen or feature plant. Excellent weeping over water. Looks good with large-leaved companion plants like *Trachystemon orientalis* or *Petasites japonicus* 'Variegatus'.

PLEIOBLASTUS (B)

A genus of huge variety ranging from the smallest bamboo (*Pleioblastus pygmaeus*) to taller leafy plants. The shorter species are valuable for garden use because of the many colourful foliage forms, being variegated with yellow, cream or white. Although evergreen and woody, many *Pleioblastus*, especially the shorter species and cultivars, generate a mass of annual growth from the base and are often seen at their best when all previous years' material has been removed. Most are spreading in habit but with occasional control the rhizomes can easily be checked to form a compact feature. Nearly all the species can be used successfully for container gardening.

PLEIOBLASTUS AURICOMUS
(SYN. P. VIRIDISTRIATUS)

Widely cultivated yellow-foliage bamboo. The long pointed pale golden leaves are variably striped green. Moderate in habit, running only when mature and moist.
H 1.5m x S 1.5 m.
Cultivation: Once established, late winter shearing or thinning will allow new colourful growth to dominate. Full sun always provides the best colour.
Uses: Underplanting for taller bamboos and shrubs. Pond-side or path edging where the colour is best appreciated. Very versatile; not out of place in a perennial border.
Similar varieties: *P. variegatus* is a high-quality variegated plan (H 1m) that is best if cut hard back occasionally.

PLEIOBLASTUS PYGMAEUS

Tiny pointed blue-green leaves on short wiry canes. Some of the leaves bleach completely in winter.
H 30cm x S 1m or more.
Cultivation: Thrives on hard pruning in late winter, or the habit is loose and leggy. Vigorous and invasive but easily controlled with a sharp spade. Sun or half shade.
Uses: Path and drive edging or very low underplanting for taller plants. Very resilient in containers.

[1] The dark foliage of *Phyllostachys aureosulcata* 'Aureocaulis' contrasts with the red or yellow stems.

[2] *Phyllostachys bambusoides* 'Castillonis' is a yellow-stemmed cultivar of a fine large-growing species.

[3] *Phyllostachys bissetii* is vigorous once established, making it suitable for screening.

[4] *Phyllostachys nigra* is the extremely popular black-stemmed bamboo.

[5] *Phyllostachys vivax* is a tidy, upright grower with a mass of thick canes.

[6] *Pleioblastus variegatus* has a reputation as one of the finest of variegated plants.

PLEIOBLASTUS SHIBUYANUS 'TSUBOI'

One of the brightest of bamboos, with pale green canes holding bunches of cream-suffused leaves. Extremely vigorous, forming a dense grove.
H 2m x S 2m.
Cultivation: Tolerant of a wide range of soils in sun or part shade.
Uses: The overall cream coloration of the foliage is best appreciated if the plant is not crowded out, so shorter foreground planting should be kept simple – try *Bergenia*, *Brunnera macrophylla* or short woody plants. Good when confined in pots.

POA CHAIXII
Broad-leaved meadow grass

Broad and flat dark green evergreen leaves make up a tidy clump that is topped by a froth of greenish flowers during May and June.
H 80cm x S 40cm.
Cultivation: Ideal for shade and even tolerant of dry soils once established. Shear hard after flowering to generate fresh foliage.
Uses: Very airy and light when in flower so it is ideal for woodland path edging or for surrounding hard landscape materials to soften the edges. Its tolerance of shade makes it an indispensable garden plant.

[1] *Pseudosasa japonica* 'Tsutsumiana' has highly ornamental swollen canes.

[2] *Sasa kurilensis* 'Shimofuri' is a cultivar with distinctive banded leaves, creating a creamy effect overall.

[3] *Sasa kurilensis*, from the Kurile Islands between Japan and Siberia, is possibly the hardiest of all bamboos.

[4] *Sasa palmata* f. *nebulosa* is one of the more invasive bamboos, but highly effective given space, or a container to limit its growth.

[5] *Sasaella masamuneana* f. *albostriata* has attractive variegated foliage and prefers sun.

PSEUDOSASA JAPONICA (B)
Arrow bamboo

Robust and vigorous species with many dark olive-green canes. Leaves are thick, large and glossy green, paler beneath. Forms a bold, vertical plant very quickly.
H 5m x S 2m.

Cultivation: Tolerant of exposure and useful in sun or shade, this is one of the easiest bamboos to establish. Runners are easy to control.

Uses: Often used as a windbreak or screen, where its performance is exemplary. Also good as a lone specimen or part of a bold planting with lower plants.

SACCHARUM RAVENNAE
Sugar grass, plum grass

Dense tussocks of hairy grey-green strappy foliage support large silver-purple feathery plumes on tall stems. Deciduous in cold climates.
H 3m (in flower) x S 75cm.

Cultivation: Full sun and warmth will produce a mass of flowers. Good winter drainage is essential if the plant is to survive. Tidy annually in spring.

Uses: A tall plant for the dry gravel garden and also useful in coastal regions. Can be used in a Mediterranean-style garden if combined with grey-leaved plants or yuccas.

SASA (B)

A distinct genus usually having large broad leaves on thin but strong canes, which often bleach on the edges during the winter, creating a variegated effect from afar. Many species provide an instant sub-tropical appearance.

Most are quickly spreading but can be successfully confined in pots, making them suitable for any garden.

SASA KURILENSIS

Incredibly tough species. Tall sheathed canes eventually turning pale yellow-green hold thick leathery leaves, which bleach slightly in winter. It provides a feeling of formality and is evenly vigorous, forming a stately grove.
H 2m x S 1.5m.

Cultivation: Sun or shade and very tolerant of exposure.
Uses: The modern approach is shady woodland edge with dogwoods or winter *Rubus*. Water-side planting with ferns and mossy rocks creates a prehistoric touch.
Cultivars: *S. k.* 'Shimofuri' has white longitudinal bands running along the broad leaves.

SASA PALMATA F. NEBULOSA

Beautiful form with fresh green canes forming dark brown blotches in sun with age. The leaves are the most exotically large of the *Sasa* species. Very vigorous, but controllable with regular digging or the use of a barrier.
H 2.5 m x S 2.5m.

Cultivation: Regular thinning of old canes and foliage as new growth commences in spring will keep the plant fresh and glossy. Tolerant of most soils in sun or shade.
Uses: For broad screening, pond-side or even in large containers. Wall planting is very effective when the leaves are striking against red brick or limewash.

SASAELLA MASAMUNEANA (B)

Similar to *Sasa* with broad, but smaller leaves. This species has a profusion of dark purple-black thin canes with a fresh display of foliage well above the ground. Spreads evenly.
H 2m x S 1.5m.

Cultivation: Can be sheared annually, otherwise thin old material as new spring growth commences. Tolerant of acid or alkaline soils and colouring better in full sun.
Uses: Groundcover or underplanting for taller bamboos. The dark canes associate well with variegated grasses such as *Phalaris* or *Holcus*, or mix with *Sasa veitchii*.
Cultivars: *Sasaella masamuneana* f. *albostriata* has good variegated foliage and a moderately spreading habit.

SCHIZACHYRIUM SCOPARIUM

(SYN: ANDROPOGON SCOPARIUS)

Little bluestem

An attractive prairie grass, invaluable for later season effect. Clumps of pale green, slightly hairy foliage change to plum-purple as the flowers develop in late summer. Flowers are pale blue-green, rapidly turning to seed as the whole plant ages to bronze and orange with the first frosts.

H 1m x S 60cm.

CULTIVATION: Versatile, thriving on a wide range of soil types and easy to establish in full sun, where it will tolerate drought. Will seed to form broad colonies, but easily controlled by hoeing. Shear annually in spring.

USES: Massed planting or ground cover with spot planting of *Miscanthus* or other tall grasses. The autumn colour is especially good with late asters, especially the dark-leaved *Aster lateriflorus* 'Prince' or the foliage of many of the new *Heuchera* hybrids.

SCHOENOPLECTUS LACUSTRIS SUBSP. TABERNAEMONTANI 'ZEBRINUS'

Zebra rush

Cylindrical rush-like leaves horizontally banded with creamy-yellow, which is often more dominant than the green. The flowers are insignificant.

H 1m x S 1m.

CULTIVATION: Needs rich, moist or wet soil in sun and tolerates marginal conditions up to 15cm deep. Needs tidying during late winter.

USES: Pool-side, for reflection in the water. Superb with night lighting as the transparency of the cream banding highlights the variegated effect.

[1] A sheath of the common, but magnificent, *Semiarundinaria fastuosa*.

[2] *Spartina pectinata* 'Aureomarginata' is a variegated grass good for large expanses of waterside where it may safely spread.

SEMIARUNDINARIA FASTUOSA (B)

A moderate runner with very stiff, erect canes, usually extremely thick, turning rich plum-purple with silver streaks as they age. The sparse fresh green foliage is dense, held on short branches close to the canes. Distinct in habit, and very hardy.

H 6m x S 2.5m.

CULTIVATION: Easy to establish in soils rich in organic matter. Sun or light shade. Prune old, thin shoots as the thicker ones emerge. Tolerant of wind, exposure and coastal conditions.

USES: Can easily be maintained as a tight clump in a smaller garden as a solitary specimen, not congested and cluttered by other plants.

SESLERIA CAERULEA

Blue moor grass

A short evergreen grass with unusual two-tone colouring. The short rigid upright leaves are dark and shiny on the upper surface and pale matt-blue on the lower side. The early spring flowers emerge purple and gradually turn to straw yellow.

H 30cm x S 30cm.

CULTIVATION: Very tolerant of alkaline soils as long as there is good moisture with some drainage. Best in full sun or very light shade.

USES: For low massed cover or edging. Excellent with dwarf spring bulbs or mixing with other short grasses.

SHIBATAEA KUMASASA (B)

Short habit with thin zig-zag canes. Very distinct, with dense mounded evergreen foliage bleaching at the tips during winter. Leaves are small and diamond shaped.

H 1.3m x S 50cm

CULTIVATION: Prefers cool, moist soil and is usually clump-forming unless conditions are very warm and wet.

USES: A fine container plant if never allowed to dry out. Feature planting by paths or patio.

SIMILAR VARIETIES: *S. lancifolia* has larger leaves on more noticeable stalks and is flatter in habit.

SORGHASTRUM AVENACEUM
(SYN: CHRYSOPOGON AVENACEUS)
Indian grass, gold beard grass

Upright and clump-forming prairie grass with pale blue-green arching leaves. The late summer flowers are a majestic shiny bronze, and dry well. The foliage turns through rich purple to orange-yellow in autumn.
H 1m x S 40cm.
Cultivation: Drought resistant and hardy, growing taller with more moisture. Adaptable to varying soil types and strong in the wind. Shear annually in late winter.
Uses: Natural planting with other prairie grasses or as a feature in the grass or perennial border.

SPARTINA PECTINATA 'AUREOMARGINATA'
Prairie cord grass

Long, arching, pale green leaves have golden margins. The flowers are not ornamental; remove them to add vigour to the leaves, which turns vivid amber in autumn and winter.
H 2m x S 1m.
Cultivation: Good, moist, fertile soil is essential or growth will be weak. Full sun sharpens the contrast of gold leaf margins against the green. Prune hard in early spring. Tolerant of exposure. Can be invasive.
Uses: Waterside planting with *Gunnera* and *Ligularia*, where it will form thickets of foliage, good for wildlife.

SPODIOPOGON SIBIRICUS
Frost grass

Highly ornamental. Stout stems have angled foliage drooping to the horizontal, giving a bamboo-like effect, Broad panicles of green-purple flowers appear in late summer. Deep rusty-brown autumn colouring.
H 1m x S 40cm.
Cultivation: Moist fertile soil, sun or light shade. Tolerant of exposure. Divide every 3 or 4 years, prune in spring.

Uses: Especially useful in the late-flowering perennial border as a foreground accent or in the winter garden outlined in frost. The architectural qualities of this grass should be highlighted and additional planting kept simple, e.g. low-growing perennials like *Bergenia*.

SPOROBOLUS HETEROLEPIS
Prairie dropseed

Arching clumps of long, hair-like, deep green leaves. Long, scented, delicate flower panicles quickly turn to seed and droop over the foliage with their weight. Turns a delicious pale chocolate-brown in autumn and winter.
H 60cm x S 80cm.
Cultivation: Established plants are very tolerant of dry arid conditions and hot sun where they show their true colour. Annual thinning and regular division will enhance the weeping appearance.
Uses: Raised beds or dry gravel gardens, or alongside paths to benefit from the scent of the flowers.

STIPA
Feather grass, needle grass

Large group of highly ornamental grasses, most tolerant of hot, dry climates. Grown for the flower/seed heads.

STIPA ARUNDINACEA

Elegant, long and narrow leaves on fountain-like clumps. The greenery turns a vivid rusty orange as summer closes. The feathery flowers arch almost to the ground and fall quickly, leaving a fiery display of foliage until the following spring.
H 1m x S 60cm.
Cultivation: Tolerant of drought and bright sun once established. Can self-seed.
Uses: Highly effective in winter combined with golden-variegated evergreens or adding colour to containers, borders or gravel gardens.

[3] *Spodiopogon sibiricus* is a herbaceous grass for the border with almost bamboo-like foliage.

[4] *Sporobolus heterolepis* is an important grass of old prairies; this species is reasonably drought tolerant.

STIPA BARBATA

Exceptional species with immensely long feather-like
seed heads that move in the slightest breeze.
H 75cm x S 60cm

CULTIVATION: Best in dry, sunny situations. Dislikes close
competition from other plants.

USES: With other dry-land, rockery and Mediterranean
plants, preferably lower growing.

SIMILAR VARIETIES: *S. pennata* is similar in habit but has
shorter seed head feathers.

STIPA GIGANTEA

Giant feather grass

Worthy of a place in any garden. The long arching grey-
green foliage supports the tall flower spikes, which are
produced late in the spring and last virtually all year.
H 2.5m x S 1m.

CULTIVATION: Restrict tidying to the autumn or winter as
spring pruning will often damage the newly emerging
flowers. Split large clumps every 4 or 5 years or flower
production will be dramatically reduced; this is best done
immediately after flowering. Discard the old central
crowns and replant the fresh juvenile growth from the
edges of the clump. Tolerant of most types of soils and
conditions including dry and exposed sites, as well as
coastal gardens.

USES: Too good to hide, so give a prominent placing. The
foliage is low and dour, so brighten up with a planting of
more colourful lower-growing plants.

STIPA TENUIFOLIA

Often called *S. tenuissima*. Tufts of very fine leaves and
silky seed heads forming cloud-like clumps.
H 40cm x S 20cm.

CULTIVATION: Any reasonable soil in sun. Short lived but
self-seeds well.

USES: Lovely *en masse*, and also when mixed with low-
growing dry-habitat plants. Effective when self-sown in
the cracks of paving.

SIMILAR VARIETIES: *S. capillata* is taller (90cm) and coarser
but its flower/seed heads create a similarly hazy effect.

UNCINIA RUBRA

Hook sedge

Deep red-brown glossy leaves arch from tight clumps. In harsh winters, the leaves may tint with orange and copper-red. Flower/seed heads are insignificant. H 45cm x S 50cm.

Cultivation: Full sun for best colour in moisture-retentive soils. Regular division or thinning of old growth is vital.

Uses: An invaluable colour in the garden. Particularly attractive with the winter colour of *Luzula sylvatica* 'Aurea' and *Carex* 'Frosted Curls', or small-leaved ivies.

Similar varieties: *Uncinia clavata* has evergreen tufts of grey-green foliage. Large club-shaped yellowish flowers turn dark brown on protruding spikes.

YUSHANIA ANCEPS (B)

A bold, running species forming large colonies of upright fresh green canes with billowing plumes of foliage arching down and outwards from the tall canes. Its beauty is best appreciated from a distance. H 6m x S 2.5m.

Cultivation: Thin old canes to produce colonies of well-spaced younger and fresher growth. Sun or shade in almost any reasonable soil.

Uses: Large landscape feature or distinct planting in parkland. Makes excellent hedging, screening and arching walkways.

Similar varieties: *Y. maling* forms a grove in time, with tall (up to 3.5m) arching stems.

[1] *Stipa barbata* is only really successful on dry soils with little competition.

[2] *Stipa gigantea* is one of the most rewarding grasses and establishes quickly.

[3] *Stipa tenuifolia* has very fine flower and seed heads that result in a cloud effect.

[4] *Uncinia rubra* has rich mahogany-brown leaves, but needs a moist soil to thrive.

[5] Masses of small leaves are a distinctive feature of *Yushania anceps*.

PRACTICALITIES

ONE OF THE WONDERFUL THINGS ABOUT
GRASSES IS HOW TOLERANT THEY ARE OF
A WIDE RANGE OF CONDITIONS. ANOTHER
IS HOW LITTLE MAINTENANCE THEY NEED.
NEVERTHELESS, THIS DOES NOT MEAN
THAT THEY WILL GROW EVERYWHERE AND
ANYWHERE, OR THAT THEY ARE TOTALLY
PROBLEM FREE. AS WITH ANY PLANTS, A
BASIC UNDERSTANDING OF THEIR NEEDS
AND HABITS WILL GO A LONG WAY.

OPPOSITE: Bamboos are definitely more fussy about
growing conditions than most grasses; shelter
from wind and a well-drained but moist soil are
essential. This is *Phyllostachys violescens*.

ABOVE: Sedges, on the other hand, are very
tolerant, especially of poor soils. This is
Carex sylvatica, which does well in light shade.

SELECTING GRASSES FOR YOUR GARDEN

How suitable a plant is for its chosen site really ought to be the most important criterion when selecting a plant. However striking it ought to look, if conditions are not right, then it will not thrive, and there is no point in planting it. Fortunately, grasses are remarkably tolerant plants, with lack of light being the chief limiting factor on what varieties can be grown. Any site that receives sun for less than three-quarters of the day during the growing season is likely to be less than satisfactory for the majority of grasses; for more shady situations those varieties that have adapted themselves for life in reduced light will need to be chosen.

Although certain species of grasses tend naturally to be found on alkaline soils, and others on acid soils, this does not mean that they have to be rigidly grown only on these soils, as is the case with many other garden plants. Grasses are tolerant of a wide variety of soil types, with only the extremes likely to cause problems. Most true grasses grow much better on fertile soils, but they flourish well enough on poorer ones, with the tough and tolerant sedges tending to be particularly successful on the latter. Consequently, there is no need for the extensive 'soil improvement' that traditional gardening has advocated (see Planting, page 105).

After light levels, soil moisture is probably the most important factor to consider. Soils that regularly suffer waterlogging should be planted only with those species known to be able to survive this – others may well rot. The same is true of soils that are regularly affected by drought; although most grasses will survive, only those from dry environments will really flourish.

Other practical considerations to bear in mind when choosing grasses are mainly to do with habit of growth. As with all plants, you should take care to ascertain the eventual height of a plant before buying. Plants in pots in garden centres are never the height they are capable of growing in the open ground. Spread is often of greater importance than height; this should be checked too. It is worth bearing in mind that some of the more popular grasses have a great many varieties in various sizes. If you adore *Miscanthus sinensis*, for example, but feel that at two metres the popular variety 'Silberfeder' is too large, there are many other cultivars that are smaller, although these might require a little more searching out from specialist nurseries.

GRASSES THAT RUN

Since some grasses are notorious for spreading rapidly, those particular species should only be planted where there is space for them. (These are indicated in the Directory, see pages 78–99.) Most spreaders are also moisture-lovers, and in any case species that run are more likely to do so on wetter soils. An exception are certain species of *Elymus*, which are dry-habitat plants; they tend to run more in light, sandy soils.

Certain bamboos are notorious runners, as can sometimes be appreciated in old gardens where they are seen to cover large areas of ground. Most bamboos run more rapidly in warm and moist climates; species that are quite restrained and slow growing in cooler areas growing at a tremendous pace. In regions that experience very warm and humid summers, great care should be taken in selecting species and in preventing their running into neighbouring property. In such climates it may be best to stick to those that are known never to run, such as *Chusquea culeou*.

Rampant species of grasses, including bamboos, may be restrained by container culture, or by growing in bottomless containers, so that the plant's main roots are in contact with the soil below them, but their horizontal running roots are prevented from spreading. Any solid barrier running down to 30 centimetres depth from the soil surface is adequate to prevent running.

CHOOSING AND SITING BAMBOOS

Bamboos have rather more specialized requirements than other grasses, needing an environment that is sheltered from strong and cold winds, both of which cause leaf scorch, and which offers consistently moist growing conditions, on soil that is well drained but never dries out. Positions in full sun should be avoided, especially outside cool temperate regions. Light woodland, slopes with water seepage and valley bottoms are the situations where the best bamboos are seen.

Bamboos do vary in hardiness, but any responsible nursery will advise on species that may not be. It would be advisable to enquire though of unfamiliar species or if you live in an especially cold area.

BELOW: Dark-stemmed *Thamnocalamus crassinoides* 'Kew Beauty' is a new cultivar of a bamboo that comes from the Himalayas. The blue colouring on its canes is unique.

RIGHT: *Pennisetum alopecuroides* is one of a genus that are very beautiful but intolerant of winter damp, tending to grow more easily in continental climates, with hot summers and cold dry winters, than in capricious maritime climates.

BELOW: Low-growing varieties of bamboo may be clipped and maintained as edging plants, as is traditionally done in Japan.

BUYING PLANTS

Most garden centres now sell a basic range of grasses, with specialist perennial and grass nurseries selling a great many more. Bamboo, being rather a cult plant, tends to be found in greatest variety in nurseries that sell nothing but bamboos.

Specialist nurseries may be located through plant directories, through advertisements in more serious gardening magazines and, increasingly commonly, on the Internet. Many, indeed most, provide a mail-order service for at least part of the year. Many also exhibit at horticultural shows, selling plants directly and taking orders. Such events are often the best way of seeing a wide variety of plants and of obtaining them.

When buying plants, either as bare root plants mail order, or in containers, it is much better to do so in spring or summer, when the plants are in active growth. Some grasses are prone to rot if they are divided outside their growing season, or if they are started into growth and then stopped. Divisions obtained in early spring should ideally be kept in a greenhouse or cold frame until early summer, to ensure that they are kept growing; a cold wet snap can curtail growth and the plants may die rapidly. Bamboos should ideally be bought as divisions of young growth, rather than old and thick canes, which will take longer to establish.

PLANTING

Traditional gardening practice lays great emphasis on soil preparation. This may be necessary for many trees and shrubs, but it is often unnecessary for perennials and grasses. A fertile soil with no obvious problems, needs little preparation. Dig a planting hole twice as wide as the plant, break up the soil at the base with a fork to loosen it, place the plant in the hole and then backfill it with soil, with any large lumps broken up. The soil level should come as close as possible to the surface of the compost that the plant had in its pot. It is often difficult to tell how deeply to plant bare-root plants, but they often need relatively deep planting to secure them. The ground around a new plant should be firmed with foot pressure to ensure good contact between the roots and the soil, and to reduce the risk of wind rock.

Soils that are particularly hard or stony should be broken up over a wider area than the planting hole, to make it as easy as possible for the young roots to move out into fresh soil. The breaking up of layers of soil below the planting position, by double digging for example, will also help. Modern practice tends to be against the addition of fertilizers or compost to soils when planting ornamental species, as some research indicates that this can sometimes do more harm than good. It is now considered more desirable to encourage plants to develop a healthier root system by making them search for their own nutrients over a wider area. Large-growing species like *Miscanthus* may well benefit from extra feeding, though.

Bamboos, being less tolerant of difficult conditions than other grasses, need more care with planting. The addition of plenty of well-rotted manure or home-made compost will enhance the moisture-holding properties of the soil – essential for success with bamboos.

Once planted, most grasses will establish quickly, reaching full height the second year after planting, although it may take several more years before some species really bulk out, particularly the *Miscanthus*. Bamboos are generally much slower to establish, they sometimes take four to eight years after planting before their full height is reached. Plentiful moisture in the first year after planting can assist greatly; these are plants that are very obviously grateful for irrigation.

MAINTENANCE

The only maintenance that most grasses require is the annual removal of dead growth. A few, notably *Molinia altissima* and some varieties of *M. caerulea*, such as *M. c. arundinacea* or *M. c.* subsp. *arundinacea*, tend to collapse in autumn, their seed heads and stems falling, which will necessitate some clearing up. Most others, though, stay firmly upright, not beginning to look ragged until the end of the winter. This time is the best to carry out tidying-up operations, cutting back last year's stems and the dead leaves of deciduous species; if this operation is left any later the emerging young growth may be damaged in the process. Evergreen sedges can also be cut back at this time to stimulate the growth of more colourful new leaves.

Those grasses that tend to run need to be looked at at least once a year, to check they are not spreading too far. Runners can be severed with a spade at the limit of where they are acceptable, and then pulled up. A few grasses can cause a nuisance by seeding prolifically, although it is difficult to predict which will do so because this is determined by the soil type, light soils often offering a more receptive seed bed. For example, some species of *Stipa* are reported as self-seeding by some gardeners, but not at all by others. If seeding does become a problem, the use of coarse mulches such as wood chip or gravel will greatly reduce it, and any unwanted seedlings that do come through can be more easily pulled out.

BAMBOO FLOWERING

Bamboos, being long-lived evergreens, require little or no maintenance. Fallen leaves should not be removed from the base of the plant, as these provide the best mulch and long-term nutrient. Old clumps can become very dense, in which case you can remove older canes to help improve the appearance of the plant – this is especially beneficial for those that have attractive canes that need to be seen at their best.

Certain problems can arise when the plants flower: which they do very rarely, usually at long intervals of decades or even centuries (some species have never flowered in recorded cultivation). The common belief *all* bamboos die after they flower is incorrect, although this does happen with some species. Flowering uses stored energy and a plant can rejuvenate strongly or die. Badly affected plants will usually produce seed, ensuring continuity; those that do not mostly recover. Simultaneous flowering of a species occurs worldwide, unless there are clonal variations, proving that all the stock of that species originated from just one source. The myth of bamboos dying after flowering has grown with the demise of *Fargesia murieliae*, but recent flowerings of other species have proved that regrowth is more usual than death. *Pleioblastus linearis, Pseudosasa japonica, Phyllostachys flexuosa* and *Yushania anceps* have all grown strongly after their flowering phase.

ABOVE: *Glyceria maxima* var. *variegata* is a marshland or waterside grass, but it can also be very effective when grown as seen here, in a container sunk into a pond.

PROPAGATION

There are two ways of propagating grasses: by seed and by division. The former method is the best way for obtaining large numbers of plants of natural species. Seed is produced by sexual reproduction, which involves a scrambling of genes, so that the offspring are all slightly different. When raising natural species (like *Miscanthus sinensis*, for example) this is no problem, but this is a problem if the plant is a cultivar, a selection whose name is enclosed in single inverted commas, like *Miscanthus sinensis* 'Rotfuchs' or *Carex riparia* 'Variegata'. There is no guarantee the seedlings will have the distinctive characteristics of their parent – seedlings of the former may not have red-tinged seed heads, the latter may not be variegated. Cultivars can only be reliably propagated by the process of division, which produces genetically identical offspring.

SEED

This is the natural way grasses spread themselves over wide areas. Many species in cultivation produce large quantities of seed that is easy to collect. Others do not set seed, or not viable seed. Some, notably bamboos, hardly ever flower and set seed. A limited number of seed companies sell seed of ornamental grasses, while growers of wildflowers for habitat restoration sell bulk quantities of seed of locally native grasses.

The seed of grasses, sedges and rushes is held in bunches, which are easy to collect, the best time to do so being when the supporting stem turns brown. The seed can usually be separated from the seed head by rubbing between the fingers. Seed should be stored in paper envelopes in a refrigerator until sowing in the spring. Not only may seed be collected from garden plants, but from plants growing wild too, although this must never be done in nature reserves or from species that are known to be rare.

Most true grasses have seeds that germinate readily in warm moist conditions, but a few, notably some species of *Melica*, *Molinia* and *Miscanthus*, need a period of warmth, followed by chilling, followed by more

LEFT: *Miscanthus* can be slow to establish, but once they are they are very long lived. This is *Miscanthus sinensis* 'Samurai'.

BELOW: *Melica transsilvanica* is a drought-tolerant grass, making it especially useful for growing on shallow limestone soils.

warmth, as do many sedges and rushes. Ideally, these should be sown in the autumn, but if not they should be sown in seed trays in spring, left in a warm place (at around 18°C) for four weeks, and then, if germination has not occurred, placed in the refrigerator at around 3°C for four weeks. Germination will occur a number of weeks after removal from the refrigerator.

Gardeners with light soil, with only a limited weed problem, can sow their seed in a nursery bed outside, covering each row of seed with a few millimetres of grit. Most will probably prefer to sow in trays of compost

however. The seed should not be covered with compost but with fine grit that allows some light through, which is often needed for germination.

Transplanting should be done before young plants become too enmeshed together in the seed tray or bed. Many are slow growing and delicate, so are best pricked out into a nursery bed or containers for the first season. Move them into final positions in late summer or the following spring, when they are in active growth.

DIVISION

All grasses and similar plants form clumps and can thus be propagated by division. Division, like taking cuttings from shrubs or perennials, is a way of reproducing plants that are genetically identical to their parents and is thus ideal for plants with special characteristics that you want to keep. The speed with which a grass forms a clump varies considerably. For example, the bamboo *Chusquea culeou*, which very slowly builds up into a clump, can only be divided after several years' growth, and not surprisingly it is an expensive plant. Running grasses like *Phalaris arundinacea* var. *picta* 'Picta' though can be divided into several new plants practically as soon as they are bought from the nursery.

True grasses that have a running habit, along with sedges and rushes, can all be divided at any time of year, but given that division is often extremely stressful for the plant since much of the root system is often severely damaged, it is better to divide in winter, when water loss is going to be minimal.

However, as a general rule, clump-forming grasses really do not like being divided in winter; several times I have seen nurseries lose their entire new stock when this is done. I myself once lost several hundred *Stipa calamagrostis* (syn. *Stipa brachytrichum* or *Achnatherum brachytrichum*) when I divided them in spring, only to experience an unseasonal cold snap the next week. In cool temperate climates, early to mid-summer, when

the plants are growing vigorously, is the only safe time. Needless to say, the young plants will need watering and possibly shading for several weeks. In regions with a continental climate, where springs are more sudden and predictable, spring is probably the best time, as plants can establish before the weather gets really hot.

Bamboos are best divided in the growing season, although this is not essential. When dividing, the top growth of bamboos should be shortened considerably, to reduce wind rock and water loss.

Established clumps or large plants may be difficult to divide. The use of two spades, inserted into the clump, back to back, to lever the plant apart, is the best way to divide such specimens. Bamboos are incredibly tough – clumps can be hacked apart with a sharp spade or axe, although this can do a lot of damage to shoots. A more precise method is to hammer a spade into the centre of the clump, much as you might use a hammer and chisel, or even to use a saw.

Divisions can usually be treated as new plants and put into their permanent positions right away. If the weather is warm and watering widely spaced plants is going to be a problem, or if the divisions are small, it might be better to grow them on in pots or in a nursery bed for a few months first of all – they can be transplanted later. Transplanting, since little root damage and no shoot damage is caused, can be carried out on any species during the autumn and winter.

ABOVE LEFT AND RIGHT: *Phalaris arundinacea* var. *picta* 'Feesey' (left) and *P. a.* var. *picta* 'Picta' are suitable only for places where their running tendencies do not matter.

GROWING IN CONTAINERS

Grasses grow well in containers. One reason for this is that they have fibrous superficial rooting systems, it being plants with long, deep-thrusting roots that adapt badly to pot culture. Those species that run, producing powerful rhizomes sideways, like some of the *Sasa* bamboos, are not suitable for long-term growing in containers, for the fairly obvious reason that they run out of space; they also make conditions difficult for any other plants sharing the container.

Grasses in containers are best grown in traditional soil-based composts, especially taller top heavy ones, which can so easily overbalance in lightweight soil-free composts. Soil-based composts are also, on the whole, less likely to become soggy and thus initiate root rot during cold wet winter weather. Very tall plants, like bamboos or *Miscanthus*, may also benefit from having gravel or stones added to the compost for the extra weight they add. Containers for tall plants need to be heavy for the same reason. All containers should have drainage holes in the bottom.

Given the vigorous growth of grasses, composts should contain a good supply of nutrients, and for the first growing season, regular feeding will be necessary. Any balanced feed is suitable, but increasing numbers of gardeners are using the long-life fertilizer granules that have recently become available to the amateur market, which need only be applied once during the growing season. Those based on Osmocote™ are the best, the resin coating being designed to allow more nutrients to be released in warmer conditions, when plants will be requiring more feed.

Frequent watering is vital, especially during hot and dry weather. Indeed, this may well be the main limiting factor in growing bamboos in containers, which are so sensitive to drought. Bamboos in containers should not be left in the sun, as both the top growth and the roots benefit from cool and shady conditions. Regular watering of bamboos is vital, as many years' growth can be permanently damaged by one failure to water.

Given that most grasses are strong growing, it is probably going to be necessary to remove and divide them every few years, otherwise the compost in the container may become so packed with roots that the plants are constantly drying out.

INDEX

Entries in **bold** refer to the Directory on pages 78–99. Entries in *italics* refer to captions.

A

Acer palmatum 'Atropurpureum' *66*
Achnatherum brachytricha *29*, *52–3*, **80**, *80*
Agrostis nebulosa 71
Alopecurus pratensis 'Aureovariegatus' 80
Amur silver grass *see Miscanthus sacchariflorus*
Andropogon species 62; *gerardii* 59
Arrhenatherum elatius ssp. *bulbosum* 'Variegatum' 73
arrow bamboo *see Pseudosasa japonica*
Arundo donax 20, 37, **80**, *80*; var. *versicolor* 35
Aster: divaricatus 68; *lateriflorus* 54

B

Bashania fargesii **80**, *80*
big bluestem *see Andropogon gerardii*
black bamboo *see Phyllostachys nigra*
blue fescue *see Festuca glauca*
blue hairgrass *see Koeleria glauca*
blue moor grass *see Sesleria caerulea*
blue oat grass *see Helictotrichon sempervirens*
bottlebrush grass *see Hystrix patula*
Bowles' golden grass *see Milium effusum*
Briza: major 22; *maxima* 11, *40*, *40–1*, 57, 71; *media* 40–1, 62, *64*, **80**, *81*; *minor* 71
broad-leaved meadow grass *see Poa chaixii*
brome *see Bromus inermis*
Bromus inermis 'Skinner's Gold' **81**

C

Calamagrostis species 19, 52, 62, 75; x *acutiflora*: 'Karl Foerster' *13*, *18*, 19, 20, 35, *38*, 42, 44, 55, *76–7*, **81**, *81*; 'Overdam' 35, 56; 'Stricta' 19, 20
Carex species *16*, 19, 25, 50, **81**; *atrata* **81**; *buchananii* 10, 58; *comans* 1, 31, 65, **81**, *81*; *dipsacea* 31, *31*, 71; *elata* 'Aurea' *52–3*, *60*, 61, 62, 70, **82**; *hachijoensis* **82**; *morrowii*: 'Evergold' 35, *35*, 71; 'Variegata' *6*, 67, 68, 70, 73, **82**, *82*; *muskingumensis* 65, 68, *76–7*, **82**, *82*; *pendula* 22, *22*, 31, 60, 68, *68*, 73, **82**, *82*; *plantaginea* 25, 68, **83**; *riparia* 'Variegata' **82**, *83*, *107*;

siderosticha 'Variegata' 35; *sylvatica* *14*, *101*; *testacea* 31, 49, 58, **82**
Centaurea dealbata 15
Chasmanthium latifolium 22, 45, 67, 68, **82**
Chimonobambusa: marmorea 67, 83; *tumidissinoda* 5, 83
Chionochloa rubra 28–9, **83**
Chondrosum gracile **83**
Chusquea species 51; *culeou* 50, **83**, *83*, 102, 108
corkscrew rush *see Juncus effusus*
Cortaderia selloana 9, 19, 20, 45, 49, 52, **84**; 'Aureolineata' 25, 34; 'Silver Fountain' *57*; 'Silver Stripe' *29*, 45
cotton grass, common *see Eriophorum angustifolium*
crookstem bamboo *see Phyllostachys aureosulcata*
Cynara cardunculus 28–9
Cyperus species *74–5*; *eragrostis* **84**

D

Deschampsia 45; *cespitosa* 30, *30*, **84**; 'Goldscheier' *69*, *84*; 'Goldtau' *12–13*, *52–3*; *flexuosa* **84**, *84*

E

Elymus species 32, 43, 58, 102; *hispidus* **84**; *magellanicus* 32, *33*, 71, **84**
Eriophorum angustifolium 60, *84*, **85**
eulalia *see Miscanthus*
Eupatorium maculatum 'Atropurpureum' *43*
evergreen grasses *16*, 19, 31, 58, 65, *65*, 67, 68, *68*, 70, *70–1*, 71

F

Fargesia species 51, **85**; *murieliae* 50, **85**, *106*; *nitida* 26, *27*, *106*; 'Nymphenburg' **85**; *robusta* 49
feather grass *see Stipa*
fescues *see Festuca*
Festuca species 25, *33*, **85**; *amethystina* 25, 32, 58, **85**; *glauca* 33, 65, 66, 85, *85*; *mairei* 15, *24*
fishpole bamboo *see Phyllostachys aurea*
Foerster, Karl 14
fountain grass *see Pennisetum alopecuroides*
foxtail grass *see Alopecurus pratensis*
frost grass *see Spodiopogon sibiricus*

G

gardener's garters *see Phalaris arundinacea*

geraniums 19, 35; *G. sanguineum* 62
giant feather grass *see Stipa gigantea*
giant reed *see Arundo donax*
Glyceria maxima var. *variegata* 86, *86*, *106*
gold beard grass *see Sorghastrum avenaceum*
greater pond sedge *see Carex riparia*
grey fescue *see Festuca glauca*

H

hairgrass *see Deschampsia cespitosa; Koeleria*
hakone grass *see Hakonechloa macra*
Hakonechloa macra 26, *27*, *52–3*, 67, **86**, *86*; 'Aureola' 34, *72*
hare's tail *see Lagurus ovatus*
Helictotrichon 43; *sempervirens* 32, *32*, 58, *59*, **86**, 87
x *Hibanobambusa tranquillans* **86**
Holcus mollis 'Albovariegatus' *64*, 74
hook sedge *see Uncinia rubra*
Hystrix patula **86**

I

Imperata cylindrica 31; 'Rubra' **87**
Indian grass *see Sorghastrum avenaceum*
Indocalamus species 26, 37, 55; *latifolius* *50–1*, **87**; *tessellatus* 35
invasive species 15, 32, 60–1

J

Japanese blood grass *see Imperata cylindrica*
Japanese silver grass *see Miscanthus sinensis*
Japanese timber bamboo *see Phyllostachys bambusoides*
Juncus effusus **87**; 'Spiralis' **87**

K

Koeleria species 15, *64*; *glauca* **87**

L

Lagurus ovatus 57, **87**
Leymus arenarius 59, 65
little bluestem *see Schizachyrium scoparium*
Luzula species 25, 65, 68; *nivea* *14*, *16*, 26, 42, 51, 68, **88**, *88*; 'Marginata' 26; *sylvatica* 65, 68; 'Hohe Tatra' *105*
lyme grass *see Elymus hispidus*

M

marble bamboo *see Chimonobambusa marmorea*

Marx, Roberto Burle 75

Melica species 22, 43, 54, 65, 67, 68, 73, 107; *altissima* 'Atropurpurea' 30, 42, **88**; *ciliata* 54–5; *macra* 42; *transsilvanica* 62, 107

Milium effusum 68; 'Aureum' *29, 34, 35, 43, 70, 73*, **88**, *88*

Miscanthus species *10–11, 19, 20, 22, 26, 37, 41, 42, 43, 43, 45, 55, 56, 57, 61, 61, 67, 75*, 88, 105, 107, 109; *floridulus 36, 37*; *sacchariflorus* 20, **88**; *sinensis* 51, 73, 75, **89**, 102, 107; 'Africa' *36–7, 54*; 'Flamingo' *38, 56, 74*; 'Ghana' *37, 41, 67*; 'Giganteus' *109*; 'Kaskade' *41*; 'Kleine Fontäne' *12–13*; 'Malepartus' *42–3, 76–7, 89*; 'Morning Light' *4, 89*; 'Pünktchen' *39*; 'Rotfuchs' 107; 'Samurai' *107*; 'Sarabande' *20*; 'Silberfeder' 102; 'Silberturm' *36*; 'Strictus' *34, 35, 36, 71*; 'Zebrinus' *35*; x *oligonensis* 'Zwergelefant' 89

Molinia species *19, 43, 45, 52, 54, 61, 75*, 107; *altissima* 106; *caerulea* 58, **90**, *90*; 'Fontäne' *44*; *caerulea* 'Variegata' *52–3*; *caerulea* ssp. *arundinacea* 10, 44, 54, 61, 106

moor grass, purple *see Molinia caerulea*

mosquito grass *see Chondrosum gracile*

Muhlenbergia japonica 'Cream Delight' **90**

muhly grass *see Muhlenbergia japonica*

N

Nassella trichotoma 14

needle grass *see Stipa*

New Zealand sedge *see Carex dipsacea*

O

Oudolf, Piet *2–3, 12–13*, 14, *52–3, 56, 62, 76–7*

P

palm sedge *see Carex muskingumensis*

pampas grass *see Cortaderia selloana*

Panicum species *10, 42, 57*; *clandestinum* **90**; *virgatum* 54, 55, **90–1**; 'Rehbraun' *90*

Pennisetum species 62, 65, 75; *alopecuroides* 71, **91**, *91, 104*; 'Herbstzauber' 75; *orientale* 50; *villosum 10–11, 109*

Persicaria amplexicaule 'Firetail' *52–3*

Phalaris arundinacea 61, **91**, *105*; var. *picta*: 'Feesey' *34, 91, 108*; 'Picta' *108, 108*

Phyllostachys **92**; *aurea* 20, *45*, **92**; 'Holochrysa' *14, 45*; 'Koi' *40, 45*; *aureosulcata* **92**; 'Aureocaulis' *21*, 93; 'Spectabilis' 13; *bambusoides* **92**; 'Castillonis' *7*, 93; *bissetii* **92**, *93*; *flexuosa* 106; *nigra* 51, **92**, *93*; *pubescens* 'Mazel' *21*; *violascens* 37, *100*; *viridiglaucescens* 47; *vivax* **92**, *93*; 'Aureocaulis' *39*

Pleioblastus **92**; *auricomus* 34, **92**; *linearis* 26, 106; *pygmaeus* **92**; *shibuyanus* 'Tsuboi' *35, 46–7, 94*; *variegatus* 56, *93*

plum grass *see Saccharum ravennae*

Poa chaixii **94**

prairie cord grass *see Spartina pectinata*

prairie dropseed *see Sporobolos heterolepis*

Pseudosasa japonica **95**, 106; 'Tsutsumiana' *94*

Q

quaking grass: annual *see Briza major; Briza maxima*; perennial *see Briza media*

R

reed grass *see Calamagrostis; Glyceria*

reedmace *see Typha*

ribbon grass *see Phalaris arundinacea*

Rodgersia 37

Rudbeckia fulgida var. *deamii* 31, 54

S

Saccharum ravennae **95**

Sasa species 37, 68, **95**; *kurilensis 6, 94, 95*; *palmata* f. *nebulosa 94*, **95**; *veitchii 14*

Sasaella masamuneana **95**; f. *albostriata 6, 94*

Schizachyrium scoparium **96**

Schoenoplectus lacustris ssp. *tabernaemontani* 'Zebrinus' **96**

Scirpus species 61

sedges 8, 31, *31*, 72 *see also Carex*

Semiarundinaria fastuosa 37, **96**, *96*

Sesleria: autumnalis 30; *caerulea* **96**

sheep's fescue *see Festuca amethystina*

Shibataea kumasasa 66, 67, **96**

Siberian melic *see Melica altissima*

silver banner grass *see Miscanthus sacchariflorus*

silver grass *see Miscanthus*

smooth-sheathed bamboo *see Phyllostachys vivax*

snowy woodrush *see Luzula nivea*

Sorghastrum avenaceum 97; 'Sioux Blue' 33

Spartina pectinata 'Aureomarginata' *96*, 97

Spodiopogon sibiricus 22, 22, 97, *97*

Sporobolus heterolepis 54, 97, *97*

Stipa species 22, 52, 59, 62, 75, 97, 106; *arundinacea* 25, 31, *31*, 97, *105*; *barbata* 98, *98*; *calamagrostis 52–3, 108*; capillata 54; *gigantea* 22, 23, 41, 44, 48, 51, 52, 54, 98, *98*; *pennata* 22; *pulcherrima* 62; *tenuifolia 13*, **98**, *98–9*

sugar grass *see Saccharum ravennae*

Sweden, James van 14, 20, 37, 62, 67, 75

sweet grass *see Glyceria maxima*

Symphytum caucasicum 43

T

Thamnocalamus species 51; *crassinoides* 'Kew Beauty' *103*; *tessellatus 66–7*

Thymus 54; creeping 33

tufted fescue *see Festuca amethystina*

tufted sedge *see Carex elata*

tussock grass *see Chionochloa rubra*

Typha species 8, *14*, 61; *laxmannii 11*; *shuttleworthii* 61

U

umbrella bamboo *see Fargesia murieliae*

umbrella sedge *see Cyperus eragrostis*

Uncinia rubra **99**, *99*

W

wavy hairgrass *see Deschampsia flexuosa*

weeping sedge *see Carex pendula*

wild rye *see Elymus hispidus*

woodrushes *see Luzula*

Y

yellow grove bamboo *see Phyllostachys aureosulcata*

Yushania anceps 26, 99, *99*, 106

Z

zebra rush *see Schoenoplectus lacustris*

SUPPLIERS

APPLE COURT
Hordle Lane
Hordle, Lymington
Hampshire SO41 0HU
Tel: 01590 642130
Fax: 01590 644220
www.applecourt.com

ARCHITECTURAL PLANTS
Cooks Farm, Nuthurst
Horsham
West Sussex RH13 6LH
Tel: 01403 891772
Fax: 01403 891056
www.architecturalplants.com

BLOOMS OF BRESSINGHAM
Bressingham, Diss
Norfolk IP22 2AB
Tel: 01379 688585
Fax: 01379 688678
www.bloomsofbressingham.co.uk

THE BETH CHATTO GARDENS LTD
Elmstead Market, Colchester
Essex CO7 7DB
Tel: 01206 822007 Fax: 01206 825933
www.bethchatto.co.uk

GREAT DIXTER NURSERIES
Northiam, Rye, East Sussex TN31 6PH
Tel: 01797 253107 Fax: 01797 252879
www.greatdixter.co.uk

JAPANESE GARDEN AND BONSAI NURSERY
St Mawgan, Cornwall TR8 4ET
Tel: 01637 860116 Fax: 01637 860887
www.japanesegarden.co.uk

PW PLANTS
Sunnyside, Heath Road
Kenninghall, Norfolk NR16 2DS
Tel and Fax: 01953 888212
www.hardybamboo.com

ROWDEN GARDENS
Brentor, Nr Tavistock, Devon PL19 0NG
Tel: 01822 810275 Fax: 01822 810275

THE SCOTTISH BAMBOO NURSERY
Middlemuir Farm, Craigievar
Alford, Aberdeenshire AB33 8JS
Tel: 01975 581316 Fax: 01975 581411
www.thescottishbamboonursery.co.uk

NURSERIES IN EUROPE

LA BAMBOUSERIE DE PRAFRANCE
301040 par Anduze, France
Tel: +33 68 61 70 47

FRIESLAND STAUDENGARTEN
Uwe Knpnadel, Husumer Weg 16
26441 Jever–Rahrdum, Germany
Tel: +49 04461 3763 Fax: +49 04461 2307

GRUGA PARK BOTANIC GARDENS
Kulshammerweg 32, D 451 49 Essen
Germany

KWEKERIJ OUDOLF
Broekstraat, 17, 6999 De Hummelo,
The Netherlands
Tel: +31 0314 381120

ACKNOWLEDGEMENTS

THE AUTHOR would like to thank Andrea Jones for her work in photographing the plants for this book and the owners of all the gardens featured, also Paul Whittaker for his work on the directory and his expert advice on other aspects of the book.

THE PHOTOGRAPHER would like to thank Russell Sharp and Phillip Brown at the Gardens of Portmeirion, North Wales; Lin Randall of the Savill Garden, Windsor Great Park; Angus White of Architectural Plants; Fergus Garrett, head gardener of Great Dixter, for his help and Christopher Lloyd for his permission to photograph; Paul and Diana Whittaker from PW Plants for their help and hospitality; Simon Trehane of Trehane Gardens; Marion Holder; Mr and Mrs Stoner; Jason Payne, garden designer (telephone 020 8969 9751); Claudia Beurer and Gerald Singel of Gruga Park Botanic Gardens; M. E Berthelot and M. M Couzet of La Bambouserie; Alan Bloom of Blooms of Bressingham; Beth Chatto; Sue and Bleddyn Wynn-Jones of Crûg Farm; John Nelson, Tim Smit and the staff at the Lost Gardens of Heligan; Hugh Angus, Tony Russell and Peter Gregory of Westonbirt Arboretum; Mr and Mrs Henry Bungener; Mr and Mrs John Lenting; Greg Redwood of the Garden Developments Unit, Royal Botanic Gardens, Kew; Dr and Mrs Marsden of Garwell House.

PICTURE CREDITS

l = left r = right t = top b = bottom c = centre

Apple Court pp10–11t, p109; Architectural Plants p14c; La Bambouserie p12t, p21l, p45tr, p47, p51cr, p61cr, p74t, p79, p112t; Terence Black p25tr, p105b; Blooms of Bressingham p31t, p58tr; Beth Chatto p34t, pp52–53b, p55l, p98 No.3; Cowley Manor pp76–77t; Garwell House p57; Great Dixter p60b, p63, p64tr, p105tr; Gruga Park p13c, p30 tr, p51r, p59tl, p65, p73b, p104; Gillian Harris p70tr; Hermanshof p15l&r, p24, p62l&r, p64bl, p107b, p112b; C. Jannsen p20, pp42–43b, p55tr, p67l; Japanese Gardens p19b, p22l, p29tr, p33t, p46, p56b, p59tr, p66t, p68l, p72, p73trl&c, p74b; Carol Klein, Chelsea Flower Show p48; Lady Farm p3b, p9, p31b, p61tr, p110; Piet Oudolf p3t, p12c, p43b, p53t, p61tl, p75b, pp76–77c&b, p111; PW Plants p6, p14br, p28–29t, p35tl, p49, p50t&bl, p67r, p70tl&70b, p71, p96 No. 1; Rowdens Gardens p35tr, p64tl; Royal Botanic Gardens, Kew p10c, p58tl, p64br, p106b; Scottish Bamboo Nursery p38t.